1

SAXON
W

Also available

The Cotswold Way
The Dales Way
The West Highland Way

RECREATIONAL PATH GUIDE

THE
SAXON SHORE
WAY

BEA COWAN

Aurum Press · Ordnance Survey

Published in association with Kent County Council

Acknowledgements

I should like to thank a number of people for their help and interest: first my husband, George, who accompanied me on most of my outings and shared the walk at every stage; Roger Lambert, Access and Recreation Officer for Kent County Council, without whose guidance and advice the project would not have been possible; Sarah Mann of the Rye Bay Countryside Project who has developed the Sussex stretch and introduced me to its pleasures; Brian Arguile who has for many years been Kent Area Secretary to the Ramblers' Association; Chris Wade of Kent County Council who negotiated the original route in its early days; Councillor Bill Davis from Lower Halstow and the many volunteers who have constructed stiles, gates and crossings and generally made the Shore Way the pleasure it is to walk.

I should also like to thank the following for their support: ADAS; The County and District Councils; English Nature, Essex, Hertfordshire and London Team; English Nature, Kent Team; English Nature, Sussex and Surrey Team; Hastings Countryside Ranger Service; Kent Trust for Nature Conservation; Hastings Countryside Park; The National Rivers Authority; The Port of London Authority; The Port of Sheerness Ltd; The Port of Dover Riverside Countryside Park; Royal Society for the Protection of Birds.

Photographs on pages 15, 18-9, 26-7, 31, 32, 42 and 120–1 are reproduced by courtesy of County Visuals, Kent County Council. The photograph on page 16 is by Roger Lambert. The photographs on pages 138 and 160 are reproduced by courtesy of the Rye Bay Countryside Project and Hastings Countryside Ranger Service respectively. All other photographs are by the author.

Front cover: *The Graveney Marshes near Seasalter*

Title page: *The south wall of the Saxon Shore fort at Richborough near Sandwich*

First Published 1996 by Aurum Press Limited,
25 Bedford Avenue, London WC1B 3AT
in association with the Ordnance Survey.

 Published in association with Kent County Council

Text copyright © Bea Cowan 1996
Maps Crown copyright © Ordnance Survey 1996

A catalogue record for this book is available from the British Library.

ISBN 1 85410 392 X
OS ISBN 0 319 00504 6

Book Design by Robert Updegraff
Printed and bound in Italy by Printers Srl Trento

CONTENTS

How to use this guide

This guide is in three parts:

• The introduction, historical background to the area and advice for walkers.

• The path itself, described in seven chapters, with maps opposite each route description. This part of the guide also includes information on places of interest as well as a number of related short circular walks. Key sites are numbered in the text and on the maps to make it easy to follow the route description.

• The last part includes useful information such as local transport, accommodation, organisations involved with the path, and further reading.

The maps have been prepared by the Ordnance Survey for this guide using 1:25 000 Pathfinder maps as a base. The line of the Saxon Shore Way is shown in yellow, with the status of each section of the path – footpath or bridleway for example – shown in green underneath (see key on inside front cover). These rights of way markings also indicate the precise alignment of the path at the time of the original surveys, but in some cases the yellow line on these maps may show a route which is different from that shown by those older surveys, and in such cases walkers are recommended to follow the yellow route in this guide. Any parts of the path that may be difficult to follow on the ground are clearly highlighted in the route description, and important points to watch for are marked with letters in each chapter, both in the text and on the maps. *Some maps start on a right-hand page and continue on the left-hand page – black arrows (→) at the edge of the maps indicate the start point.* Should there have been a need to alter the route since publication of this guide for any reason, walkers are advised to follow the waymarks or signs which have been put up on site to indicate this.

FOREWORD

The Saxon Shore Way is one of the Recreational Routes planned to help walkers to get the most out of the network of paths which link settlements across the English countryside. The Way makes use of footpaths, ancient tracks and dykes, mainly on existing rights of way, to make the route as pleasant and convenient as possible. The Shore Way has been developed by Kent County Council and East Sussex County Council with funding from the Countryside Commission.

This well-researched Guide helps you to plan your walk whether you decide to undertake the whole Way, a distance of some 160 miles, or to spend a day exploring one particular section.

The Saxon Shore way is especially rich in historical associations. The many historic buildings along the Way all have stories to tell, and this Guide will stimulate your imagination as you trace the footsteps of past inhabitants, from stone-age man to industrialists and famous artists and writers. Should you need rest and refreshment many of the historic old inns along the Way will provide it, as they did for travellers before you.

The marshes which fringe the Saxon Shore are renowned for wildlife, particularly wading birds. The skies are often filled with the sight and sound of the endless migrations which cross and re-cross the seas. Migrating birds as well as a great variety of native species find food in the rich mud and vegetation of the marshes.

The Saxon Shore Way, with its towns, villages, farms and stretches of estuarine wilderness, exemplifies the conversation between man and nature which has made the English landscape. Bea Cowan's excellent Guide invites you to take part and enjoy it.

Sarah Ward

Countryside Commissioner
Kent County Councillor

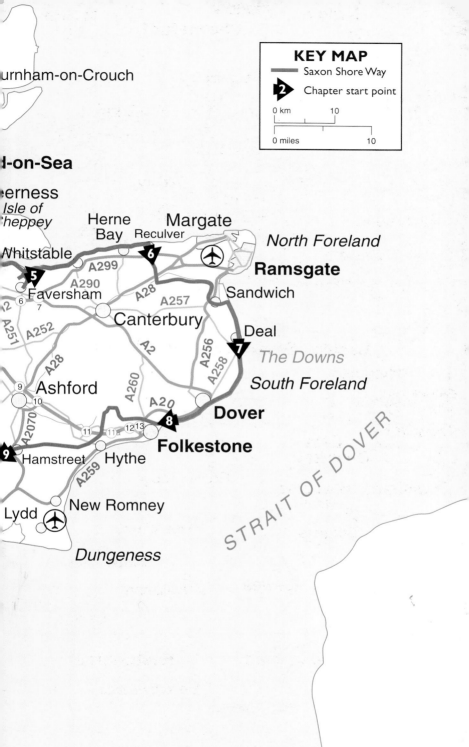

urnham-on-Crouch

KEY MAP
Saxon Shore Way
2 Chapter start point
0 km · · 10
0 miles · · 10

d-on-Sea

eerness
*Isle of
heppey*

Herne
Bay · Reculver
Margate

North Foreland

Ramsgate

Whitstable

A299

5

A290

Faversham

6

7

A2

A251 · A252

A28

A257

Sandwich

Canterbury

Deal

A256

A258

The Downs

7

Ashford

A260

A2070

A20

8

9

10

11 · 11a · 12 · 13

Dover

Folkestone

9

Hamstreet · Hythe

A259

New Romney

Lydd

Dungeness

South Foreland

STRAIT OF DOVER

DISTANCE CHECKLIST

This list will assist you in checking your progress along the walk.

Location	Approximate distance from previous location	
	miles	**km**
Gravesend	0	0
Cliffe	7.5	12
Hoo St Werburgh	7.5	12
Lower Upnor	2.5	4
Strood Station	2.5	4
Gillingham Station	3.5	5.6
Strand	1.5	2.4
Otterham Quay	5	8
Lower Halstow	3.5	5.6
Kingsferry Bridge	6.5	10.4
Sittingbourne Stn	5	8
Conyer Quay	6.25	10
Harty Ferry	3	4.8
Oare	2.5	4
Faversham	3.5	5.6
The Sportsman Inn	6	9.6
Whitstable Harbour	4	6.4
Herne Bay	4.5	7.2
Reculver	4	6.4
Plucks Gutter	7	11.2
Richborough Fort	6	9.6
Sandwich Quay	2	3.2
Deal Pier	5.5	8.8
St Margaret's Bay	5.25	8.4
Dover (A2)	3	4.8
Aycliff	2	3.2
Folkestone, Crete Road East	4.5	7.5
Etchinghill	5.5	8.8
Saltwood	2.75	4.4
Lympne	2.25	3.6
Aldington	5.5	8.8
Hamstreet	4.75	7.7
Appledore	4.5	7.2
Rye	7.5	12
Winchelsea	3	4.8
Fairlight	3.5	5.6
Hastings	4.5	7.2

Handwritten annotations: 1st (Cliffe), 2ND (Hoo St Werburgh / Lower Upnor), 16ml (Gillingham Station), 3RD (Lower Halstow), 17ml (Kingsferry Bridge), 15¼ (Harty Ferry), 4th (Oare), 5th / 14½ (Whitstable Harbour), 6th (Richborough Fort), 7th / 14 (St Margaret's Bay), 8th (Folkestone), 9th (Aldington), 10th (Rye)

INTRODUCTION

The Sarre Penn, one of the many drainage dykes built by the monks of St Augustine's Abbey, still dissects reclaimed marshland near Chislet.

THE SAXON SHORE

South-east England boasts a rich and varied landscape. From the wild expanses of the North Thames marshland to the intimate patchwork of wealden wood and ghyll, from saltings and estuary to ancient chalk downland, the diversity is immense. Even the cliffs boast a variety of structures and rock forms. Two areas of this countryside, the North Downs and the High Weald, have been designated as Areas of Outstanding Natural Beauty. The Saxon Shore Way leads the walker through all this varied landscape and provides an exhilarating and fascinating introduction to the history of the area and an insight into the way such a landscape developed.

The Saxon Shore Way was originally opened in 1980. Now re-established, and in parts re-routed and extended, it takes the walker for some 160 miles round the coast of Kent from Gravesend to Hastings in East Sussex. It follows the coastline of the South East as it was around 1500 years ago, long before the North Kent Marshes or the Romney Marsh came into existence, when the cliff lines to north and south extended further into the sea and when the Wantsum Channel provided a thoroughfare for boats between the Isle of Thanet and mainland Britain.

The Way takes its name, the Saxon Shore, from a line of fortifications built along the coastline as it was in the third century AD, towards the end of the Roman period. This was a time of crisis when several of the tribes bordering the Roman Empire were threatening the frontier. In Britain these incursions largely took the form of pirate raiding, although some of the attackers may simply have been looking for land to settle. These invaders, generally known as Saxons, came from the southern regions of modern Denmark, and could travel rapidly in long-ships which also could penetrate far inland up the many estuaries and creeks.

In response, the Romans built or strengthened a line of forts to repel the incomers; first at Brancaster (*Branodunum*) on the Wash and at Reculver (*Regulbium*) on the north coast of Kent, and later at Richborough (*Rutupiae*), Dover (*Dubris*), Lympne (*Lemanis*) and Pevensey (*Anderida*). Three others have been identified at Bradwell (*Othona*), Burgh Castle (*Gariannonum*) and Portchester (*Portus Adurni*). Sometimes, as at Richborough and Dover, the forts were built close to the sites of the ports which had long served as points of entry to Britain or which, like Dover and Lympne, already provided a base for the regular Roman fleet, the *Classis Britannia*. Elsewhere the forts were erected at sites where there was believed to be an immediate threat. The remains of the forts have been excavated and some, at Richborough, for example, are at least partially standing.

The term 'Saxon Shore' first appears in a list, *Notitia Dignitatum*, which reviews all the commands and postings of troops throughout the Roman world and refers to the 'Count of the Saxon Shore' (*Comes Litoris Saxonis per Britannias*), a position whose origins are obscure, but one that was obviously of some importance in the twilight world where the historical record of Roman Britain begin to fade into the so-called Dark Ages.

GEOLOGY AND LANDSCAPE

The landscape seen along the Saxon Shore Way is part of what is known to geologists as the Wealden area, from the High Weald which rises at its centre. Little is known of the underlying rock foundations, but what is visible of the geology from different points along the route provides a fascinating insight into the landscape's development.

Around 160 million years ago the last of the Jurassic rocks were being formed. At this time south-east England alternated between swamp and savannah and iguanodon still roamed the land. Over the next 40 million years, during the early Cretaceous period, rivers deposited successive layers of sandstone and clay. These accumulated and solidified, until eventually their weight caused the central area to subside, allowing the sea to enter.

During the following 10 million years marine deposits were laid down to form, first, the Lower Greensand, then the Gault clay, then the Upper Greensand. After this, crustacean deposits accumulated to form a dense chalk layer. Then, around 100 million years ago, huge earth movements, probably connected with those which created the Alps, pushed the centre of the area upwards into a dome almost 3000 feet (1000 metres) high. Weathering from wind, rain and ice immediately began to erode the crest of the dome, while on the outer, initially the lower, slopes of the dome, the chalk remained to form the basis of the

Downs. In places chalk was eroded to reveal the Greensand and the Gault. The centre was further eroded to expose the sandstone.

Three main rivers drained the slopes, though their courses were very different from today. The Medway drained the northern slopes of the High Weald cutting its way through the chalk of the North Downs. The southern slopes were drained by the Rother. The third river, the Kentish Stour, flowed eastward from the Greensand slopes near Ashford.

Later, around 45 million years ago, in the Palaeocene and Eocene periods, the sea again took hold, laying down a series of pebble beds set within deposits of clays, loams and sands, in what was to become the Thames Basin. Later still, wind-blown loess, or brick-earth, settled in patches on the northern slopes.

One of the fascinations of the Shore Way is the chance to see the different strata which underpin the landscape. In effect, you walk from the latest to the oldest. To the north of the Downs, beside the Thames and the Medway and alongside the Swale, you see the familiar grey-blue London clay of the Thames, mud never to be ventured on, for its fine particles cling and hold unrelentingly. Further east, the cliffs at Bishopstone Glen show in profile the various muds, clays and pebble beds from the Eocene period, compacted into their distinct strata.

Sheep graze in traditional style under the apple trees in the North Kent fruit belt near Sittingbourne.

Vipers bugloss, bird's foot trefoil and sainfoin - an array of wildflower species typical of chalk grassland at Langdon Cliffs in early summer.

From Kingsdown to Shakespeare Cliffs between Dover and Folkestone, the white chalk rears up in splendid dignity. There is a break in the chalk near Folkestone where the cliffs are formed out of the Gault clay, the layer between the two Greensands; this is Folkestone Warren which is slipping, it is thought, on the surface of the chalk. At Peene quarry, in the Downs behind Folkestone, you can see the tiny crustacean deposits that formed the chalk. Gault cliffs appear again at Lympne where the Saxon Shore fort has all but vanished through the movements of the earth. Finally, first on the Isle of Oxney, next at Houghton Green Cliff, east of Rye, at Rye itself and at Friars Cliff beside Winchelsea, then from Cliff End to Hastings, rise the sandstones of the High Weald, typically known as Hastings Beds.

Such, in outline, is the geology old shoreline. Today's coastline is very different, and many of the changes have occurred only in the last few thousand years. Most dramatic was the final separation of Britain from the European continent in about 5000 BC when the North Sea broke through to form the Straits of Dover. Other changes have come where land has been lost through weathering and erosion, a process still evidently affecting the chalk cliffs near Dover, the Gault near Lympne and the softer clays of the Eocene period as well as the sandstone of the Hastings Beds.

Elsewhere land has been gained from the sea, above all the marshland. In the south, the Romney and the Walland marshes now stretch where as recently as 12000 BC sea lapped against the sandstone cliffs. Gradual sinking of the land led to the first accumulation of silt deposits; the land rose to become moorland and forest, sank, then rose again. By the turn of the era the Rother flowed into a broad, tidal estuary, emerging at the point where the Romans established the port of *Lemanis*. Much of the mouth was already protected by a shingle bar. From then on, alluvial silt brought down by the river combined with the steady drift of pebbles and shingle along the Channel coast from west to east to create marshland. Soon men started to drain the marshes, a process which was completed by the seventeenth century. Today the cliffs, separated from the sea by mile upon mile of arable and pasture, are a distant but evocative reminder of landscapes long vanished.

Another area greatly changed is the Wantsum Channel to the east of Canterbury. This was a tidal channel, almost a third of a mile (500 metres) wide, separating the Isle of Thanet from the mainland, It was flanked by stretches of saltmarsh which were covered by water at high tide. In early medieval days it provided a good route from the English Channel to the Thames estuary. Over the centuries, the channel steadily silted up as mud was driven in from the North Sea. At the same time people began to 'in' the marshland, protecting it with sea walls and draining it to provide arable and pasture. The same process

St Thomas' Church, Fairfield stands in marshland typical of the Romney and Walland

Marshes where sheep graze and the dykes are a haven for wildlife.

of 'inning' accounted for the creation of much of the north Kent marshland where wattle fences were erected from the eleventh century. Today as you walk east of Cliffe on the Hoo Peninsula you can discern the old cliff-line almost as clearly as you see it above the Romney Marsh between Hamstreet and Appledore.

Much of the development of the landscape is linked to the woodland cover which developed from around 8000 BC when birch and willow began to spread from central Europe, to be followed by Scots pine, hazel, oak and elm. Alder and lime arrived in lowland England in a warmer period, around 4000 BC. This led eventually to the creation of a dense forest which covered the entire South East. Much of it survived into Roman times, to be known as *Silva Anderida*, the Anglo-Saxon *Andredsweald*, the wood behind Pevensey, the Roman *Anderida*. But from neolithic times, around 5000 to 4000 BC, the ancient forest began to be denuded, slowly at first, more rapidly later, as people settled the land and the development of the landscape became in large part an interaction between men and nature.

The first clearances took place as men felled trees, to build dwellings, for grazing, and later for pasture and arable land. Woodland on both chalk and sandstone was cleared in this way very early on, creating the downland to be seen near Dover and Folkestone and the heath above Hastings. Other areas were felled for houses well into the Middle Ages, and after that for ship-building.Coppiced woodland, a distinctive feature of the South East is much in evidence, especially on the Gault clay near Saltwood. Coppicing, which developed from early on, involves felling timber and leaving the stump or 'stool' intact. From this, within a few years, several new trunks will grow.

Other changes came as men utilised the resources in the ground. Iron in the clay below the sandstone attracted Celts to the Hastings area; brick-earth beside the Medway was used by the Romans for tiles and bricks; salt was panned and collected after evaporation beside the North Sea and beside the Wantsum Channel; chalk was quarried along the Downs; mud, clay, chalk and gravel were excavated from the nineteenth century onwards around the Hoo peninsula for the manufacture of 'Portland' cement. Ragstone was extracted from quarries at Folkestone, Hythe and Sandgate. The quarries became part of the landscape and nature adapted itself to them.

The old buildings of Kent and Sussex reflect the materials to hand. The oldest to survive are the fine half-timbered houses, their oak studs and braces infilled with plaster. You will see many of these along the Way. As timber supplies dwindled, people looked to other resources, and new materials came into fashion – first weatherboarding, then

The Dutch Gable of St Peter's Church reflects the influence of Huguenot
settlers who came to Sandwich in the sixteenth and seventeenth centuries.

hung tiles and, above all, brick. Bricks, easily sourced and beautifully
fashioned, supplied many needs. They also proved to be all the natural
medium for the distinctive style of architecture, noted for its 'Dutch
Gables', introduced into east Kent in the sixteenth century when
Huguenots settled there as refugees from France and Holland.

The soils over such a wide area obviously varied in fertility, the rich
clays proving the best for agriculture, the downland and heathland providing excellent grazing land. The clay on the chalk slopes running down
to the Swale and to the River Medway nurtured the fruit introduced first
by the Romans, then again by the Normans and finally reintroduced in
Tudor times. Hops, introduced from the Low Countries, became a feature of this countryside from the late fifteenth century.

A sprit-sail Thames barge rests in the saltings beside the River Medway near Hoo St Werburgh while the spars of another are etched on the skyline.

WILDLIFE

Most of the wildlife habitats in the South East have been created by the interaction of man and the environment. A walk along almost any part of the Saxon Shore Way will give ample opportunities to observe birds, plants and invertebrate life. You pass through a remarkable number of Sites of Special Scientific Interest (SSSIs) as well as several of the even more significant National Nature Reserves, such as Hamstreet Woods, while the Thames estuary forms one of the most important designated areas in the country. It is well worth taking binoculars and at least a small notebook, if not a pocket reference book. No place is without its own interest, but a number of sites stand out, if only because of the fragility of the local environment and the risk of it being destroyed by development.

North Kent Marshes

The North Kent Marshes were created by man in the first instance, when existing mudflats and salting were 'inned' for extra grazing. Over many centuries, regular winter flooding followed by evaporation in spring and summer created grazing marsh of an unusually brackish nature. The resulting plant life is rare in this country. On the saltmarsh you will find plants adapted to this harsh environment such as eelgrass, glasswort and sea lavender, which provides a mauve carpet in late summer. The dykes and fleets have their own flora, which is encouraged where possible by regular clearance. In brackish water you may find the delicate brackish water crowsfoot. In fresher water you may find soft hornwort or golden dock. Throughout the grazing marsh you will also find a great range of moths and butterflies.

Nearby in the estuaries the thick, clinging mud supports over a hundred species of worms and molluscs. These attract wildfowl to such an extent that the Thames estuary, the Medway and the Swale form the most important estuarine habitats for birds in the UK. It is an unforgettable experience to see the flocks of migrating birds which pass through the area in hundreds of thousands over a single season. As well as residents such as redshank and plovers, you may expect to see, during the winter, visitors from the arctic regions such as wigeon and brent geese as well as visiting rarities such as avocets.

Two areas of the North Kent Marshes, the Swale and The Medway Estuary and Marshes, have been designated 'Wetlands of International Importance' under the Ramsar Convention. They are also 'Special Protection Areas' under a European Directive ('The European Community

Directive on the Conservation of Wild Birds'). The Thames estuary and marshes are being considered for both designations.

But this landscape has already changed much over recent years. After the floods of 1953 most of the sea walls were rebuilt and with the sea permanently excluded the salinity of the water has changed. Intensive farming over the last 40 years has converted much grazing marsh to arable land while new developments for leisure always threaten.

Chalk Grassland

The unimproved grasslands of the chalk downs make an exceptional habitat for wild flowers, arguably the best in Europe. You may find up to 40 species in one square yard (one square metre). Rare orchids are just some of the endangered species of which survive here. You will also find vetch, rock rose and knapweed, among others. Once again, the habitat is endangered, for several reasons: the age-old practice of grazing sheep, which first created the grassland, has died down allowing stronger, tougher grasses to grow which smother the delicate flowers. Nearby the typical trees and shrubs of chalk grassland, dogwood, guelder rose, hawthorn and ash smother the plants even more. Far worse, where even a single dressing of fertilizer has been applied, the plants' root systems are destroyed.

Typical signs of unimproved grassland are the hummocky anthills left by generations of ants. Where newer hummocks have been left by sheep or cattle you will find that welcome efforts have been made to reintroduce summer grazing to maintain the ideal height of grasses.

Walland Marsh and the Pett Levels

The marshland between the landlocked cliffs of Stone in Oxney and Fairlight Cove is another area with strong wildlife interest, containing several SSSIs and including areas proposed for SPA and Ramsar status. The intricate network of sewers, the open ditches which helped to drain the land, has removed almost all the salinity from the soil and so created a variety of mainly freshwater habitats.

Today the ditches are intensively maintained by the National Rivers Authority (NRA). This work, done outside the nesting season, enhances the conservation intererst since plants vary as the dykes are cleared. You may find the rare soft hornwort as well as the more common marsh mallow and ther fi=ringed water lily. In the rare stretches of brackish water you may still find the brackish water crowfoot. The area is rich in insects including a wide range of dragonflies and damselflies. The whole area is a haven for migratory birds. The Rye Harbour Nature Reserve is another important area which deserves a visit.

Hastings Country Park

The high ground between Cliff End and Hastings is another important area for conservation, as much for its geology as for its wildlife. Like Bishopstone Cliffs near Reculver, Warren, Fairlight and Ecclesbourne Glens are unique in the south east for the strata they reveal. Here, as you cross each successive glen, you can see the different layers of sandstones laid down throughout the early Cretaceous period. The strata are as crucial for what they tell of the history of the rocks as for the traces they reveal of mesozoic life – insects, molluscs, reptiles such as crocodile, turtles and dinosaurs, as well as early mammals. The glens, especially Fairlight Glen, are damp, moist areas. Beside the streams which tumble over the rocks you will find ferns, lichens and mosses which are survivors from a warm, wet era, known as the Atlantic period, between 5500 and 3000 BC.

The trees in the woodlands on the slopes vary according to the altitude, changing from oak, ash, and hazel on the slopes, to alder beside the streams. In the moist clays you will find dog's mercury and the violet helleborine. On the high ground at Firehills heathland was created by grazing sheep; since grazing ended this has given way to bracken and the gorse, which blazes yellow in late summer, grows in abundance. Even so, you may still find ling and bell heather or even occasionally dog violet or fenugreek. Work is underway to restore this important habitat further and you are asked not to walk in fenced-off areas.

SETTLEMENT

The earliest Stone-Age men settled in Britain from as early as around half-a-million years ago. Some traces have been found at Swanscombe, near Gravesend; more have emerged beside the Medway estuary, on the higher ground above the present River Stour, near Folkestone and Dover, and above Hastings. Until the connecting land disintegrated and the English Channel was formed around 5000 BC, people wandered freely between the two land masses.

After this any arrivals from Europe to Britain assumed the role of true settlers, who left their mark on the countryside in distinctive ways in several places along the Saxon Shore Way. One area settled from around 4000 BC was the stretch of land behind Folkestone. From about 2000 BC another wave of settlers arrived, known from the earthenware they produced as the Beaker People. Their remains have been found above Kingsdown. Then from 500 BC came Celtic immigrants

At Harty Ferry beside the Swale the tide ebbs to reveal mudflats and saltings whic

...re inhospitable to people but rich in invertebrate life.

who introduced the use of iron, and cultivated the land further, so accelerating the decline of the ancient forest. Traces of their fortifications have been found at Dover and on the East Hill above Hastings.

The Roman occupation after the invasion of Claudius in AD 43 was a period of reasonable calm and prosperity. Gradually Celts and Romans intermarried and trade generally prospered. Roman villas stood at the centre of farming or trading areas. The Painted House at Dover and the villa on the East Cliff at Folkestone are only two of over 40 in this area. Above all a network of communications, the Roman roads, was established, linking towns and other large settlements.

That period of calm finally came to an end when the Romans withdrew in order to concentrate their forces nearer to home. Old texts describe a period of chaos and confusion, couching their accounts of the end of an era in terms of catastrophe and apocalypse. The turmoil came as much from the economic chaos left behind by the departing Romans as from the incursions of new peoples. These people, generally categorised as Angles and Saxons, came from different parts of Northern Europe. The early settlers in Kent came from Jutland and Frisia. Their settlements have been found beside the Swale at Milton Regis, near the modern Sittingbourne, at Chatham, and beside the Wantsum Channel. Kent was soon quite densely colonised and was the first Anglo-Saxon kingdom in England to became established.

Saxon settlement took longer in Sussex, the land of the South Saxons. The difficult terrain of the High Weald and the dense woods, still unfelled, formed an almost impenetrable barrier, and groups remained isolated for much longer. The *Haestingas*, who gave their name to the Hastings area, were only brought into a wider grouping when the Mercian king, Offa, defeated them in 771. Not long after, in 786, the kingdom of Kent also fell to Offa. From then on the South East was under a single ruler.

This unity may have helped the spread of Christianity, officially introduced to England by St Augustine after his landing in 597 at Ebbsfleet, then an island near the mouth of the Wantsum Channel. Augustine was welcomed by King Ethelbert, whose Frankish wife was already a Christian. He was granted freedom to preach and to use the church of St Martin at Canterbury which had been founded in Roman times. He was consecrated bishop within the year and his many activities soon led, in 604, to the consecration of Justus as Bishop of Rochester. After Ethelbert's death Christianity took some time to become established, even in Kent, while in Sussex it took almost 100 years for it to penetrate. But the results were momentous for society as well as for individual souls.

The coming of the church brought England into greater contact with Europe, it encouraged the development of laws and resulted in the establishment and growth of the important abbey of St Augustine's (first dedicated to St Peter and St Paul) at Canterbury, and the monastery of Christ Church.

The monks of Canterbury were also important to the area throughout later Saxon times and the Middle Ages because of their role in developing agriculture and fisheries. Acquiring land throughout Kent, often through gifts from local landowners, they were responsible for much of the 'inning' of marshland, both on the Hoo peninsula at Cliffe, and along the Wantsum Channel. Subsequently, a number of monastic houses grew up, as at Minster-in-Thanet, Dover and Folkestone as early as the eighth century, and later still (under the Austin Canons), at Bilsington.

When the Normans defeated Harold's men in 1066 at Senlac, six miles from Hastings, little was done to change the structure of society. Rather society was strengthened. More settlements grew and over the next 250 years more timber was felled for house construction than in any such period before or since. The Shore Way passes through comparatively few areas of woodland. What there is lies mainly on the Gault and Greensand in the south. It is significant that most of the ancient woodland was felled before the Middle Ages.

DEFENCE OF THE REALM

From the time the North Sea breached the land-bridge with the European mainland right up to the Second World War this part of England has always seemed vulnerable. With the thin, grey line of the French coast only 22 miles away at its nearest point, defence of the south-east coast has remained a crucial priority for successive governments as the remains of Iron-age forts, Norman keeps, Tudor castles, the Thames and Medway defences, and concrete pill-boxes, all testify.

One historic defensive system was the Confederation of the Cinque Ports, a grouping of five towns active from the eleventh to the sixteenth centuries, which were deemed capable of providing the King with ships and men to watch the English Channel and transport soldiers to the continent when required. The original five towns were Hastings, Romney, Hythe, Sandwich and Dover. Later Winchelsea and Rye were added. Smaller towns, such as Faversham were considered 'limbs'. Members of the Confederation had rights as well as duties, above all the exemption from taxation and the freedom to conduct their own affairs. Such status gave considerable impetus to the growth of all these towns.

The Napoleonic Wars saw the construction of two other features of the south-eastern landscape, the Martello Towers and the Royal Military Canal. A string of Martello Towers was built to defend the Kent and Sussex coast between 1805 and 1808. To reinforce these strongpoints, on the instructions of William Pitt, the Prime Minister, it was decided to dig a canal from Sandgate near Hythe to Cliff End. The canal was started in 1804 and, though never fully completed, filled with water in 1806. Part of it was based on navigable stretches of the River Tillingham and the River Brede between Rye and Winchelsea. Beside it ran the Royal Military Road. One feature of the canal is its numerous turns, or enfilades, designed to offer defenders the opportunity to catch an invading army in a cross-fire as it attempted to cross the obstacle. In the event the French army of invasion never came and the canal was used for some time for commercial traffic. Today it has become a major habitat for wildlife.

ART AND LITERATURE

The landscape of the South East has inspired many writers and painters. The marine artist W.Wylie lived at Hoo for most of his working life; J.M.W. Turner committed many scenes from the area to canvas, from Chatham and the River Medway to the dramatic sea and sky at Hastings, painted in the 1830s. The Pett Levels near Winchelsea were the setting for Sir John Millais' 'The Blind Girl'.

An even greater variety of writers is associated with the region. Perhaps Julius Caesar started the trend with his account of the area in the *Gallic Wars*. In 1570 William Lambarde wrote the first history of Kent and Edward Hasted wrote his *History and Topographical Survey of Kent* in 1885-95. William Cobbett in his *Rural Rides* made sharp comment on many of the places on the route of the Shore Way in Kent and Sussex. William Shakespeare's description of the cliffs at Dover in *King Lear* will endure as long as the English language, while Joseph Conrad provided a memorable description of the Thames at Gravesend in *Heart of Darkness*. One place, perhaps, stands out above the rest, Rye, home of many writers and artists, such as Henry James, Conrad Aiken, E.F. Benson, Rumer Godden and Radclyffe Hall.

But when one looks for literary associations, there is one writer who, above all, comes to mind – Charles Dickens. Dickens spent six years of his early childhood in Chatham where his father worked in the Naval Pay Office in the dockyard. No 2 Ordnance Terrace, now No 11, where

The ragstone keep at Rochester Castle, guardian of the River Medway for nearly 1,000 years, looks over the river to slopes once quarried for their chalk.

The slips, roofed over in the nineteenth century, formed the industrial heart of Chatham's historic dockyard.

the family lived for some of that time, can be seen near the Shore Way and many of the places passed on the walk figure in Dickens' work.

Chatham features as the first meeting place of Mr Pickwick and Mr Wardle. It also appears in *Seven Poor Travellers* and *David Copperfield*. The churchyard of St James', Cooling, on the Hoo peninsula, is described evocatively, with swirling mist and night descending fast, as the meeting place of Pip and the convict Magwitch in *Great Expectations*. Rochester features many times, in *Pickwick Papers, The Mystery of Edwin Drood* and in *Great Expectations*. In *Bleak House* Esther Summerson visits Edward Carston who is stationed at the Royal Marine Barracks in Deal, while Dover became home to David Copperfield's aunt, Miss Betsy Trotwood, and provides the natural setting for Jarvis Lorry to meet Lucy Manette in *A Tale of Two Cities*.

Dickens' work evokes endless scenes which can still be seen today. Indeed, a walk along the Saxon Shore Way could be devoted to these places alone.

Preparing for the Walk

The success and enjoyment of your walk around the Saxon Shore Way will depend as much upon the planning as on the walk itself. For this you will find the Useful Information at the end of the book helpful: a Select Bibliography gives suggestions for background reading; for those who wish to walk the route in longer sections or in its entirety there are some recommendations for finding accommodation and the list of Tourist Information Centres will point to more; for those who would like to linger in an area, a list of circular walks helps you to explore different facets of that region. Another section lists features, whether buildings or centres of wildlife interest, which are worth exploring if you have the time.

The book is divided into ten chapters. Each chapter covers rather more ground than many people will wish to attempt in one day, but each deals with a geographical area which forms a unity in itself. Each chapter begins and ends at a point where you will conveniently be able to join or leave the Shore Way, and there are other such points within each chapter. In general, the route can be subdivided into stretches of roughly ten miles each, sometimes more, sometimes less. The Shore Way is never impossibly far from local bus services, though

'Pip's Graves', the lozenge tombs in the churchyard of St Thomas' Church, Cooling; the setting for the opening scenes in Dickens's Great Expectations.

The Royal Native Oyster Store in Whitstable overlooks the Horsebridge, the slipway

...here horses pulled carts to and from the sailing craft at the water's edge.

you should check beforehand the times of day, and even the day of the week, these function, especially at weekends. In most places you can link with a satisfactory railway line. If you find there is no such easy link it is worth using a local taxi service, generally not expensive. Another possibility is to combine the use of a car with the railway network, using a train to return to your car at the end of a day's walk.

Plan the day's walking carefully and do not underestimate the time it takes to cover a stretch of the route. This is lowland country, but must be respected nonetheless. The marshland may be flat but is often hummocky. There are few hills, the cliffs at Kingsdown, Shakespeare Cliff and the glens of the Hastings Country Park being the exception to the rule. Two miles per hour makes a good average, and allows you to view the scenery as you go. You should also allow ample time to link with public transport if you plan to use it.

Take adequate clothing both for warmth and for protection against the rain. This may be south-east England and not the Cairngorms but the wind can be bitter along the north Kent coast in winter, and it blows just as vigorously beside the cliffs to the south east and south. Good waterproofs and an extra jersey are essential. Boots are also recommended, even for meadow and marshland, as much for the support they give to ankles as for coping with muddy areas. Good maps, kept in a waterproof pouch, will complement those in this Guide, and a compass should always be carried in case a mist closes in. Take the normal first-aid supplies. Also take adequate food and drink. Pubs are shown on the maps and often indicated in the text, but it is always possible they may be closed.

Except in urban areas, where there is no waymarking, it has not been necessary to describe every right or left turn along the route or to refer to every stile, kissing-gate or bridge. Once you are on the walk you will find that the signing and waymarking for the route is excellent throughout. The waymark for the Saxon Shore Way is unmistakeable, the logo of the Saxon raider's horned helmet engraved within an arrow, red, yellow or blue according to the status of the route at that point. All arrows give a very accurate line to follow and distinguish the Way from any other coincident route. The route description in the text gives the essential directions and a general account of the way to go. The maps allow the walker to follow the directions with confidence.

Inevitably, there are areas where urban development, tarmac and concrete, even caravans, have taken hold, but these are surprisingly few and far-between considering you cover more than 160 miles through the most densely populated corner of England. They can be

from there to the pier you will see a mural depicting the water-men's riot of 1833. The watermen had achieved importance from the Middle Ages as men skilled in operating the flat-bottomed boats which took passengers and goods out to the boats anchored in the channel. The mural depicts their violent objection to a new pier which threatened to undermine their livelihood.

From here you walk eastwards and, almost immediately, pass The Three Daws, 600-years-old and notorious for its smuggling past. Go down the steps above St Andrews church to the Royal Terrace. Here you will see on your left the remains of a Tudor blockhouse and beyond that the Royal Terrace Pier.

Turn right, then left, then left again by the Custom House **2**. HM Customs has had long-established links with Gravesend, dating back to 1299 when Searchers were appointed to check goods brought by sea. This fine Regency building was built in 1814 for what was then the Excise Department and became the centre for HM Customs and Excise London Port Collection in 1991.

Now turn left into Commercial Place and walk through a large gateway past the walls of the New Tavern Fort and the site of the

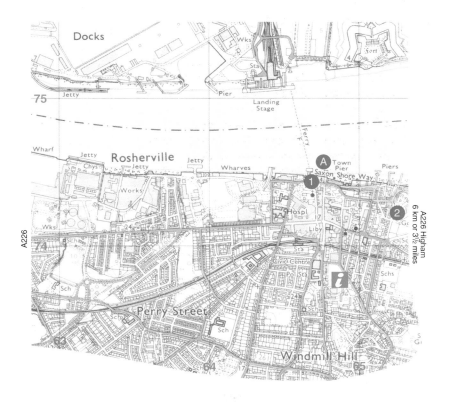

The antennae, masts and funnels of the Port of London Authority tugboats fill the

twentieth-century skyline on the Thames at Gravesend.

Milton Chantry. You now come to the Gordon Promenade **3**. This is named after General Charles Gordon who, as Royal Engineer Officer in Command from 1865 to 1871, commanded the Fort here. He was killed in the Sudan in 1885, and is known to history as Gordon of Khartoum.

Here for the first time you come close to the River Thames and have views both upstream and downstream. From Celtic times the Thames has seen trade between Britain and Europe. Early exports included slaves, dogs, corn, cattle and metals, which were exchanged for ivory, amber and glassware. The river grew in importance as the ports at Lympne and Richborough, which you will visit further along the Way, silted up. Today the Port of London Authority, (PLA), is responsible for all the tidal stretches from Teddington Lock to the mouth of the estuary off Margate. The river is still the busiest waterway in the country and now you see freighters carrying coal, aggregates and paper to the wharves at Gravesend and Northfleet, while container ships pass upstream on their way to the Dartford International Ferry Terminal by the Queen Elizabeth Bridge.

Occasionally you can see the traditional sprit-sail barges of the Thames and Medway pass by. During the annual race from Gravesend to Pin Mill in Essex they make a glorious sight.

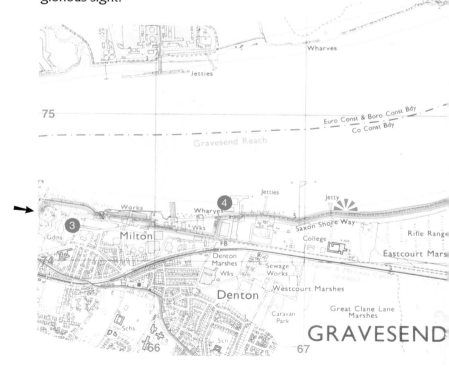

GRAVESEND

At the far end of the Promenade go up to the road beside the canal basin, then over the lock gate into Albion Parade. After 100 yards (90 metres) turn right and follow a narrow path to Wharf Road. At the end turn left and follow this road round to Denton Wharf **4**. Follow the sign to the Fish and Lobster, a welcoming pub where you can read some fascinating accounts of the river's history.

Climb up steps, turn right and walk along the sea wall towards the Hoo Peninsula. Soon you have open views towards the edge of the North Downs. Closer by, you will see the tower of St Mary the Virgin's church at Chalk **5**. The sea wall provides a good, often breezy, vantage point from now on, with views across the marsh and down the estuary. One and three-quarter miles (3 km) along the wall you pass Shornmead Fort **6**, built by General Gordon.

Pass the light **B**, then, 600 yards (550 metres) further on, drop down to the lower wall beside Higham Saltings **7**.

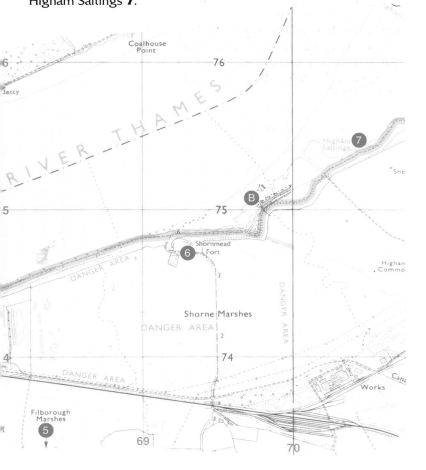

Here a ferry may have operated up to the early middle ages before the Thames channel ran deep. Continue towards the old gravel pit **8**, one of the many excavated when the cement industry flourished here and now a busy sailing area, then turn left towards Cliffe Fort **9**, another nineteenth-century defence work. Skirt the fort, passing old jetties, then walk along a metalled track and go under a con- veyor belt onto a cinder track beside the sea wall. After 200 yards (180 metres) the path forks left beside Cliffe Creek **C**.

To the north, beyond the creek, stretches traditional grazing marsh. Once used to produce and store ammunition, it is now an outstanding breeding area for birds, though much threatened by development.

Higham saltings provides a good point from which to view old and new sea traffic where the Thames widens into the Lower Hope Reach.

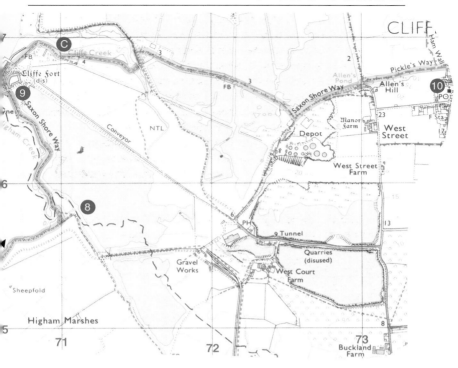

You can see a windpump and St Helen's church, Cliffe **10**, above the face of an old quarry ahead to your left. As you walk round the head of the creek you see the line of refineries at Thameshaven in Essex. Turn right over a packed-rubble ramp over a wall and walk ahead for three-quarters of a mile (1.2 km) along another cinder path flanked by lagoons.

Turn left when you see the buildings of a small oil depot ahead and walk beneath the old quarry-face to the foot of Allen's Hill. Two quick turns left, then right, take you to Pickles Way where after about half a mile (800 metres) you turn right past a farm and walk up to the village of Cliffe **11**. The Black Bull stands on the corner of Reed Street. One hundred yards (90 metres) along Reed Street is a village shop.

From the middle ages Cliffe belonged to Christ Church, Canterbury. The monks grew barley and grazed sheep on the marsh until the late fourteenth century. The town provided one vessel when called upon by Edward I so it must have had a small fleet and the many additions to St Helen's church reflect some of the wealth of the area.

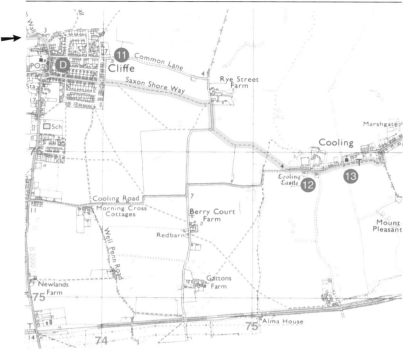

Go ahead, past the Black Bull **D**, then, when the road bends right, continue straight on to Swingate Avenue where you turn left. At the end, cross the road and go ahead into fields. The path now takes you along the edge of the old cliff line, with the land sloping down northwards towards Cliffe Marshes where, in winter, you will see endless flights of wildfowl on the move.

Turn right at Rye Street Farm. At the next corner, turn half-left to a stile, walk along the side of a field to a footbridge, then turn half-right and go diagonally across the next field to the road. Turn left, past Cooling Castle **12**, a manor house fortified by John de Cobham in 1381, and head towards St James' church **13**.

Here in the churchyard, where the young Pip meets the convict Madgwick in Dickens' *Great Expectations*, lie a collection of tiny, lozenge-shaped body stones. In reality there are thirteen but Pip claims five, 'sacred to the memory of five little brothers of mine'. They are a permanent reminder of the marsh fever, or ague, now better known as malaria, which plagued the peninsula right up to the latter part of the nineteenth century.

Take the path to the south of the churchyard to a farm track, turn left, then right, on to the road. The Castle and Horseshoe lies 200

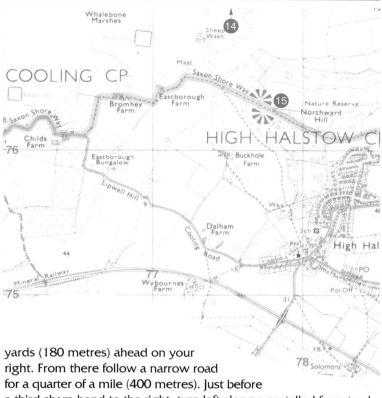

yards (180 metres) ahead on your
right. From there follow a narrow road
for a quarter of a mile (400 metres). Just before
a third sharp bend to the right, turn left along a metalled farm track
through a pear orchard. Turn right through Bromhey Farm and then
left at a junction of farm roads, to go through Eastborough Farm.
Just before a mast, turn right and follow the path leaving a willow-
lined ditch to your right. Turn right over a wooden bridge and climb
up the slope to the edge of woods.

From a well-placed seat, just before a short flight of steps, you
can absorb an outstanding panoramic view west up the Thames
estuary. To your right, the north, you can see Decoy Fleet snaking
its way across the marshes to Egypt Bay, the remote spot once
notorious for the prison hulks which used to be anchored there **14**.

The Way now continues through the woods of Northward Hill **15**.
This important reserve, run by the Royal Society for the Protection of
Birds (RSPB), is home to Britain's largest colony of grey herons who
come to nest between March and May. Woodpeckers have a busy
time in the old oaks and you might just hear nightingales, even in
daytime.

Below Northward Hill the Hoo Peninsula stretches to the River Thames.

Follow the path for half a mile (800 metres) to the far side of the wood, then turn left into a field just north of High Halstow. Here you get your first glimpse of the River Medway.

Now walk on to Decoy Hill Road, another fine vantage point. You see the church of St Mary's Hoo ahead, now private dwellings **16**. Turn right at the road and go ahead to another field path. After 250 yards (230 metres) turn right down Bessie's Lane, a delightful green lane which winds gently downhill to the road at Fenn Street.

Turn left, then right, to cross the A228, a busy highway leading to Thamesport on the Isle of Grain. Go up the lefthand side of a garage and follow a lane, then the side of a field, until you reach a right turn along a private drive **E**.

Where the metalled road turns right, follow the track ahead, first between trees then between fields. You can see Rochester and Chatham on the far side of the Medway.

Cross the mineral railway **17** which runs from Higham to the Isle of Grain. At the road go straight across the next field, then turn left just beyond a large tank. At the next road turn left, then right after a few paces, and walk beside a pear orchard to a solitary house 550 yards (500 metres) ahead **F**.

Between this point and Lower Upnor **G** you have a choice of routes, either along the edge of the Medway, or over higher ground.

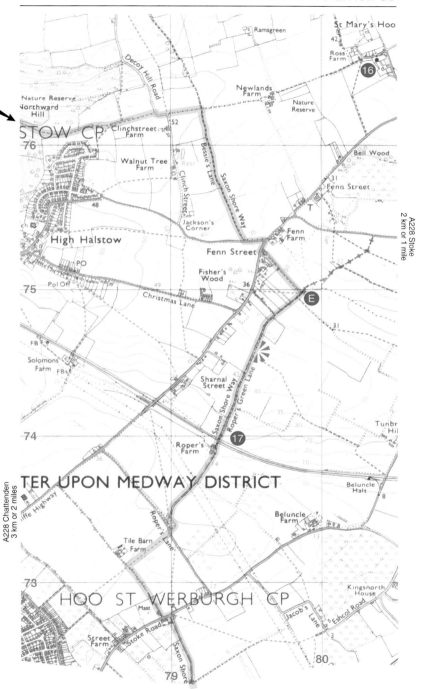

St Mary's Hoo

Ramsgreen

Ross
Farm

16

Newlands
Farm

Nature
Reserve

Decoy Hill Road

Nature Reserve
Northward
Hill

STOW CP
76

Clinchstreet
Farm

52

Bell Wood

Walnut Tree
Farm

Bessie's Lane

Saxon Shore Way

Clinch Street

31

Fenn Street

48

T

Jackson's
Corner

Fenn
Farm

ch

High Halstow

Fenn Street

PO

Fisher's
Wood

Pol Off
75

Christmas Lane

49

36

E

31

FB

Solomons
Farm

FBs

Sharnal
Street

Saxon Shore Way

Roper's Green Lane

47

40

35

30

74

Roper's
Farm

17

26

Tunbr
Hil

TER UPON MEDWAY DISTRICT

Beluncle
Halt

8

iffe Highway

Roper's Lane

Beluncle
Farm

Tile Barn
Farm

73

HOO ST WERBURGH CP

Kingsnorth
House

Mast

Jacob's Lane

Eschol Road

Street
Farm

Stoke Road

Saxon Shore

80

79

A228 Stoke
2 km or 1 mile

A228 Chattenden
3 km or 2 miles

The shoreline from Hoo Marina is not passable within an hour either side of high tide so please check the time and the state of the tide before venturing on the shore route, then allow some more time for extra safety and more still for enjoying the riverside. It is two and a half miles (4 km) along the shoreline itself and from **F** the whole stretch to Lower Upnor is half a mile (800 metres) longer than if you go by Hoo St Werburgh. Tide-tables for Rochester are available locally from W.H. Smith.

All this being equal, to follow the shoreline go ahead from **F** to the edge of the river. Kingsnorth Power Station **18**, three-quarters of a mile (1.2 km) to your left downstream, stands on the site of a station where airships were built in the First World War. Ahead, on Hoo Island stands, Hoo Fort **20**, built in the nineteenth century to improve the defences of the Medway. Turn right and walk along the sea wall beside marshes to the beginning of boatyards, then go down from the sea wall and follow the path to a road at the entrance to Hoo Marina. Follow the sign through the fence and, keeping to the fenced path, come to open ground leading to the beach. Now walk along the beach below Cockham Wood **19**.

When you come to the end of the beach, go up on to the shore-line beside the Medway Yacht Club and then ahead to the road. As you reach Lower Upnor you pass the training ship *Arethusa* **22**, the fourth in a line first started by the Shaftesbury Homes in 1873. Here go ahead along the Upnor Road.

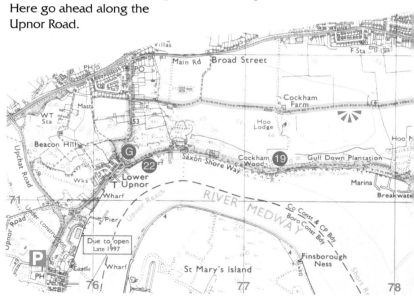

If you choose the upper route you have the chance to stop at Hoo St Werburgh to see the church and for shops, a pub and buses to Strood and Rochester. It also offers, further on, some of the best views you will ever have of the Medway at Rochester.

For this upper route turn diagonally right across the field at **F**, then right again towards Hoo St Werburgh. A track runs south on your left, just before the road, should you wish to join the shore route. At the road turn left and then right to skirt the church of St Werburgh **21**. Go on to the far side of the churchyard, then along a lane to an open field. Here turn left, then right, along a metalled road. At a metal gate just before Cockham farm it is worth looking back for a fascinating view of old and new: Kingsnorth Power Station, Thamesport in the middle distance and Grain furthest north, with the spire of St Werburgh nestling between them.

Go through Cockham Farm, then ahead for nearly three-quarters of a mile (1.2 km), enter a narrow path beside houses, then walk on to Elm Road. Turn left. A few yards ahead you can see Rochester and the River Medway with the M2 road bridge in the distance. Beside a small car park alongside Beacon Hill go ahead into the woods and follow the path downhill to a metalled track beside houses. One hundred yards (90 metres) ahead you reach Lower Upnor **G**.

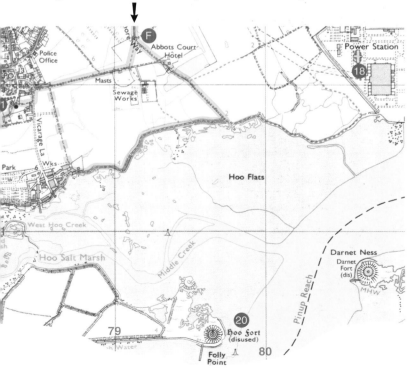

Turn right. Now walk along Upnor Road for a quarter of a mile (400 metres). Cross the road to the gates of the Royal School of Military Engineering. Continue to the bend and go left up a flight of steps to reach Upchat Road. The King's Arms stands at the corner of the High Street.

The High Street, with white weather-boarded houses running down to the Medway, must be one of the smallest streets so named in the country. Go down to the river's edge and you will find Upnor Castle **23** beside the river on your left.

By the mid-sixteenth century the Medway had become increasingly important as a haven for the Royal Navy. Upnor Castle was built between 1559 and 1565 to help to protect the fleet anchored there. It did not see action until the Dutch fleet's daring raid upon the anchorage in 1667.

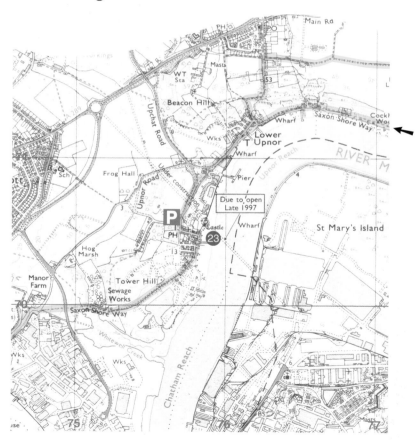

Upnor Castle, built beside the River Medway in Tudor times, today looks out over gentler craft than the men-of-war it was once intended to repel.

2 THE MEDWAY TOWNS

Upnor to Gillingham Strand 7½ miles (12 km)

The wide mouth of the Medway estuary has always been an area of mudflats, sand and winding creeks. People found a livelihood here from the earliest times, coming to fish or hunt and later to dig clay for pots. It was not until well into historic times, in the Tudor period, that the area acquired strategic importance. The Medway became a haven for ships, the shores were used for shipbuilding and saltmarsh was reclaimed for dockyards. The quarrying of chalk, clay and brickearth, combined with this naval role, created a lively local economy and people's presence, has done much to change the landscape, sometimes several times over.

The next six to seven miles (10-11km) of the Saxon Shore Way, from Upnor to Gillingham Strand, are almost entirely built up. But there are many vantage points from which to view the shoreline and, with old Rochester as a centrepiece, the area's historical legacy is immensely rich.

From Lower Upnor you can either take a bus from the Upnor Road or walk the next one and a half miles (2.5 km) to Strood. The walk is mainly on metalled paths, fringed with light industry, on the reclaimed land of the Frindsbury Peninsula. Nearer to Strood the area is currently derelict but to the historian of the Medway even this part is intriguing.

Turn right at the waterfront beside Upnor Castle **A** and walk along the river's edge below houses, then follow the path half-right through a wooded area. Go left to skirt MoD property and walk to a road. Cross, go up steps, then turn left along a metalled road, Upnor Road. Where this turns right and becomes Parsonage Lane, you should take a steep, narrow path down the side of the old Frindsbury quarry. Bridge Reach lies ahead, with Rochester beyond.

Rochester Castle stands proud beside the river. The city's cathedral nestles behind. To your right is Strood, well supplied with churches. St Nicholas **1**, with a Norman tower, watched the town grow from a small settlement beside the main road to London. St Mary's **2**, the one with the spire, followed in the nineteenth century when Strood had added barge-building and quarrying to its earlier fishing activities.

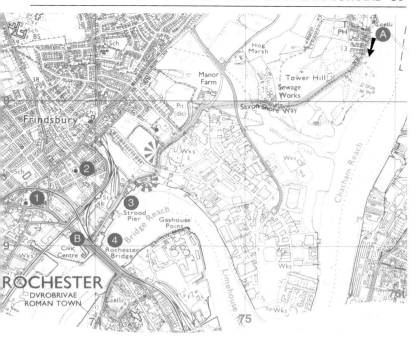

Cross the next road and start down a road leading to works, then, almost immediately, fork right, still downhill, along a narrow path until you come to old sheds in Canal Road **3**.

Once the centre for barge-builders and corn merchants, the road actually takes its name from the old Thames and Medway Canal which, in 1809, had been cut through the hillside to Higham, to create a shorter and, in times of war, safer route to the Thames. The canal proved a costly failure. Abandoned in 1845, the channel was filled in and used for railway track. Strood Station, built in 1854, stands on marshland filled with chalk excavated for the canal.

Continue to the High Street **B**, cross and turn left towards the Rochester Bridge **4**. While you consider the castle on the far bank, you may also marvel at the complexity and number of the nearby bridges.

Little is known today of the town the Romans founded on the far bank. Even the name, *Durobrivae*, is lost; the name Rochester coming from the writings of the Venerable Bede who called it *Hrofaecaestre*. What is known is that the Romans established a wooden bridge on the present site. Its foundations were discovered in the mid-nineteenth century. Before the Romans came, only a ford upstream provided a crossing over the Medway. What peaceful days!

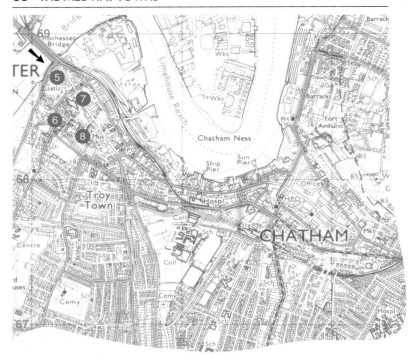

A Saxon bridge replaced the Roman one in 960. That, in turn, was replaced by a fourteenth-century bridge 40 yards upstream. Then came a Victorian replacement, designed by William Cubitt, back on the original site. The bridge you now cross, going from west to east, was built between 1911 and 1914 on the site of Cubitt's bridge. Since the middle ages Bridge Wardens have had the sole authority to bridge the river.

The story behind the east-west carriageway is also part of railway history and recalls the days before railway companies found it advantageous to amalgamate. The London Chatham and Dover Company, formerly the East Kent Railway Company, opened the first railway bridge over the river in 1860. In 1892 the South Eastern Railway, which had run from London to Strood since 1844, opened its own line to run alongside. The two companies amalgamated in 1899 and closed the earlier line in 1911. The foundations of this earlier line stand beneath the steel box-girder construction of the east-west carraige-way, built over them in 1970.

Once across, you turn right opposite the Norman Conquest public house. Here you walk beside Gundulph Square towards the

Esplanade. The Bridge Chapel on your left commemorates the builder of the late medieval bridge, Sir John de Cobham, who had it built as a chantry for perpetual prayer.

On the corner facing you is the entrance to the Castle **5**, built in Norman times to protect the town by Gundulf, the Bishop of the time; Gundulf was consecrated bishop in Rochester in 1077. The cathedral is his chief legacy but in 1088 he also built the stone castle **5**, one of the earliest in the country. You still see part of his walls on this, the west side. The towering ragstone keep, the tallest in the country, was built by a successor in 1127.

Now follow the Centenary Walk sign past Castle Hill and the castle, then turn left past the castle up Bakers Walk.

On the right you see Satis House, which once belonged to Richard Watts who oversaw the building of Upnor Castle and built the Poor Travellers House in the High Street. Elizabeth I is said to have exclaimed 'satis', (enough), in thanks for his hospitality.

Now turn left onto Boley Hill, and look at the west door of Gundulf's cathedral **6** and the tympanum, where Christ sits in glory in the centre. The figures of Justus and Ethelbert stand on either side. These are thrilling works of Norman sculpture which sum up both the history and the intent of this lovely place. Justus was one of St Augustine's fellow missionaries, ordained here by his leader in 604. King Ethelbert, who had welcomed St Augustine to his shores, built a church for him. Soon the church became his cathedral. Gundulf's rebuild, of 400 years later, deserves as long a visit as you can manage.

Charles Dickens' presence appears throughout in the town he immortalised as Cloisterham. If you walk further down the slope you reach College Gate, with weather-boarding above and ragstone below. In *The Mystery of Edwin Drood* this became Jasper's Gatehouse. Turn right into the High Street **7**, and you find the Watts Charity for the six poor travellers, basis for *The Seven Poor Travellers*. Further along, Eastgate House was to become both Westgate House in *Pickwick Papers* and the Nun's House in *The Mystery of Edwin Drood*. Today the Charles Dickens Centre occupies Eastgate House. In the garden stands Dickens' chalet, brought from his house at Gad's Hill, Higham.

Return to Boley Hill, and walk along Minor Canons Row just beyond, that is south, of the cathedral, then past the Deanery and the King's School, Mackean House. Leave Oriel House and The Archdeacon's House on either side, enter the Vines **8**, a delightful small park, once the monks' vineyard, and walk across to the far righthand corner.

Ahead, slightly to the left, stands Restoration House. Here Charles II stayed on his way to London to be crowned king after exile in France. Samuel Pepys also stayed here when visiting the dockyard at Chatham, though he was more interested in the ladies than the house. Renamed Satis House, this was where Miss Haversham lived in *Great Expectations.*

And now some walking. Cross Crow Lane, then go down East Row, and ahead up Gravel Walk and St Peter's Path. Turn left into King Street, with The Rising Sun on the far corner. Now cross Delce Road to Star Hill. Turn right and make your way uphill to the roundabout. Cross the City Way **C** at a central reservation just above the roundabout, turn right up the hill, then turn left into the park and recreation ground. Walk above the tennis courts and the bowling green towards the College of Art and Design. Between the Georgian houses of New Road you have glimpses of Chatham's docks and Chatham Reach.The route swings left, then turns right, onto a rubble side-road and climbs to Fort Pitt Hill. Over the hill to your right stands Fort Pitt Grammar School **9**. Fort Pitt was the site of the principal military hospital in the early nineteenth century and was later chosen by Florence Nightingale to be the first Army Medical School.

Turn right for a few paces, then left, still across the park, with a superb view of the Medway. The road to your right becomes Ordnance Terrace **10** where Dickens spent his early years.

Turn left opposite Boundary Road and pass the bandstand, then go right, down a paved slope to New Road. Cross carefully and go steeply down Hammond Hill, between the premises of the Ancient Order of Foresters and the Unitarian Church. Turn right into the High Street, Chatham now, then go left into Medway Street. At Sun Pier **11** you can pause for another fine view down the Medway. Go on to Globe Lane, turn left, then take the road signed to Gillingham going uphill, left. The Town Hall is unmistakeable on the right.

If you wish, you can walk to the Riverside Gardens, just before the turning, to reach Command House, a good pub, well situated, as its name suggests. You climb steps just beyond it to reach St Mary's church **12** and return to the Shore Way in Dock Road, just above Globe Lane. The church, now redundant, houses the Medway Heritage Centre. Cross at the traffic lights outside the church from where a side road leads up the hill to Fort Amherst **13**. This remarkable fortification was built between 1765 and 1803 to protect the dockyard below. The Fort covers over 36 hectares, complete with ditches, revetments, powder magazines and a network of tunnels linking them all.

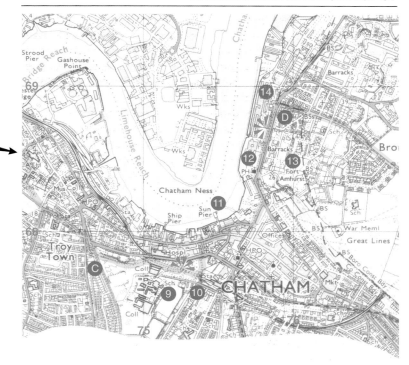

To continue, take the raised path above Dock Road for 600 yards (540 metres), where a view of the Medway compensates amply for the traffic below.

Ahead on the left is the old Royal Dockyard, Chatham **14**, closed in 1984. The outer basin is now used by the Medway Ports Authority, while the middle basin is open to the public. Warships were built here before the Spanish Armada but the dockyard first grew to fame in the seventeenth century when the Dutch navy threatened Britain's command of the Channel. HMS *Victory* was launched here in 1765, as was *Achilles*, the first 'Ironclad', in 1863. The site gradually lost its importance due to shoaling in the Medway. The architecture is as interesting as the history. You will find Classical revival and Palladianism at its best, in Admiral's House, built 1704, and the oldest naval building in the country. Officers' Terrace was built in 1727. There is also the splendid Store Department with its clock dating from 1802. The Ropery, Hemp Store and Tarring House are just as intriguing.

Just before the Dockyard, turn right **D**, up The Cut, to reach Brompton and go ahead along Pleasant Row and Garden Street. Here you find a grid of narrow streets, built in the eighteenth century

This sixteenth-century house beside the Vines in Rochester once welcomed Samuel Pepys to stay and later became the fictional home of Charles Dickens' jilted, mad Miss Haversham.

to house the troops who protected the Dockyard. Prospect Row, right, and Mansion Row, left, are pure Georgian. There are numerous pubs in this area, as you would expect. As you continue the names of the streets recall their military past.

Follow the signstone along the Sally Port ahead. Soon you pass the large open space, the Great Lines **15**, the northern edge of the eigtheenth-century fortifications. An area of old chalk grassland, it has escaped building and harbours the rare red star thistle.

At the far end turn left along Marlborough Road. Continue to the The Viscount Hardinge public house and turn right into Gillingham High Street. This is a pedestrian area, with street markets and a bustle of buying and selling. Leave the railway station to your right, continue down Railway Street and turn left into Kingswood Road. Turn right **E** over a disused railway and walk ahead down Parr Avenue from where Thamesport seems but a stone's throw away.

Watch for Corporation Avenue on the left and turn half-right opposite it, along Church Path on the slope below some open space. At the end turn left, into Church Street, then right into Gillingham Green. There are superb views here from Church Path of Upnor, and, from Church Street, of Hoo.

This is the oldest part of Gillingham, an airy, elevated spot. Gillingham parish church, dedicated to St Mary Magdalene **16**, was founded by the Normans and developed over the centuries. The dockyards, cement- and brick-making came later to the slopes.

Leave the church to your left, walk down the churchyard slope and pass the Victorian House on Grange Road, also on your left. Follow the road left, then enter the cemetery. Leave a terrace of houses to your right, then turn left along a concrete path. Turn right at St Andrew's Methodist church and walk down a narrow, walled lane. Across the Medway you see St Werburgh's, Hoo. At the bottom of the lane go down steps, cross the road at the central reservation and follow the path ahead leading to Gillingham Strand.

3 THE MEDWAY TO THE SWALE

Gilingham Strand to Sittingbourne   *20 miles (32 km)*

Gillingham, once a small fishing village, grew rapidly in the nine-teenth century. The dockyards spread downriver from Chatham, while the quayside was thronged with barges taking bricks from the brickyards on the slopes. Although the waterfront has clearly changed, you can still imagine some of this activity as you walk beside Gillingham Marsh.

The Shore Way continues beside the Medway, passing creeks and inlets. The harder rock stands out as islands and peninsulas surrounded by the thick, blue-grey alluvium typical of this estuary. In the nineteenth and early twentieth centuries it gave the 'mud-dies' and clay-getters a good living as they toiled to load their barges in between the tides. Today it gives waders and wildfowl a rich source of food by hosting the invertebrates they eat.

The Medway estuary and marshes, classed as an SSSI, provide wonderful habitats for wintering wildfowl, which are drawn here not only by the mud but also by the wide variety of grasses grow-ing in saltmarsh, reedbeds, scrub and sand dunes.

Navigation on the Medway estuary and the Swale is controlled by the Medway Ports Authority. Only a relatively narrow channel beyond the saltings is completely navigable but you will see small boats in most of the creeks and inlets. Sheerness at the mouth, on the Isle of Sheppey, is the largest terminal but you will see vessels making for docks at Chatham and Gillingham, St Mary's Island and Ridham beside the Swale, as well as Thamesport.

Turn down the approach to the Strand Leisure area **A** and fol-low the path to the riverside. Ahead you can see the nineteenth-century Hoo Fort **1** and Darnett Fort **2**. Kingsmill, Thamesport and Grain dominate the horizon. In the middle distance the Medway is usually studded with small boats.

Follow the path to Owen's Way. Here turn right, then left, round factories, following the footpath signed to Motney Hill. At the riverbank turn right and skirt the edge of Gillingham Marshes for one mile (1.6 Km) until you reach the entrance to the Riverside Country Park, then skirt the Eastcourt Meadows, a haven for wild flowers and butterflies.

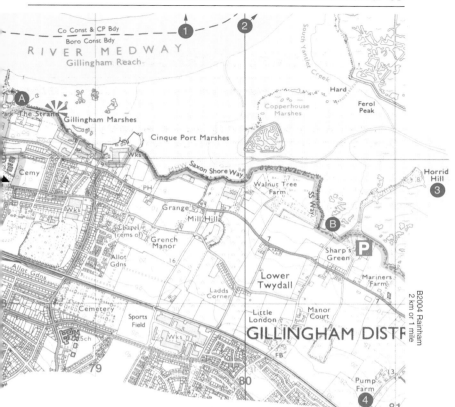

Ahead is Horrid Hill **3**, linked to the mainland by a causeway that once carried a small railway to cement works on the island. It takes its name from the conditions French prisoners endured aboard hulks moored here during the Naploeonic Wars.

Cross a car park **B** beside Sharps Green Bay, then go between shrubs, beside Sharps Green Pond. To your right, beyond a second car park, a Visitors' Centre provides interesting background to this important wildlife area.

You now walk along a broad track beside Rainham Creek. At one time this was, like most places along the shores, busy with shipping, with three quays in operation. Rainham itself, on the A2, the old London-Dover road about a mile to the south, has a fine church, St Margaret's **4**. Nearer to the shore, barely three hundred yards (270 metres) away, runs the old road from Chatham to the King's Ferry. It still has several inns should you require a break.

You pass Bloor's Wharf, the only quay still active, where freighters unload scrap metal. The biggest of the docks **5**, was used by cement works. The mud was brought in sprit-sail barges from nearby marshes. The huge hulk lying here was the *Athena*, towed in after being wrecked off the south coast.

Turn left just before the road and walk towards the small rise of Motney Hill **6**. Beyond the path are important reedbeds and saltings, maintained by the RSPB, which attract hundreds of birds in season.

Turn on to the road and follow it towards the entrance to the sewage works. Turn right over a stile just before the entrance, go left to skirt the field, then right and ahead, to the wall above Otterham Creek. Here turn right, following the creek wall to a fenced path. Continue until you reach a stile and turn left, then right, to walk through the works to the road. Turn left past Otterham Creek boatyards **C**.

Barges were built here, then used to transport bricks from the nearby brickfields and for cement. After about 30 yards (30 metres) turn left up a narrow path to orchards.

Here follow the signs to the far righthand corner.

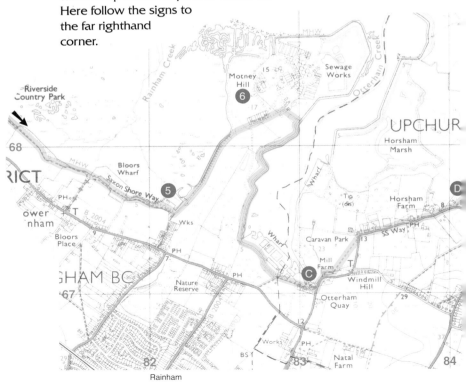

Sharps Green in the Riverside Country Park, where a causeway leads to Horrid Hill.

Go down to the road and walk for half a mile (800 metres) along a narrow road. You pass a pub, The Brown Jug, on your way. This was once the route from Chatham to the King's Ferry, so many will have stopped here before you.

You pass Horsham Park, an impressive house with dormer windows and hung tiles, then the Shore Way turns left over a stile **D**. If you continue along the road you reach Upchurch **7**. St Mary' church is unusual, with a two-tiered shingled spire. Here Sir Francis Drake grew up. His father had been driven from the West Country in a Catholic uprising and, after a spell living in a hulk on the Medway, settled here as Rector.

Meanwhile the Shore Way takes you above Horsham Marsh and then leads through orchards to the road at Wetham Green. Here turn left, then, after 300 yards (270 metres), right, to walk along a lane on the right-hand side of a field. Follow the Saxon helmet signs sharp right and then left, and continue along a lane and up the lefthand side of an orchard to the road at Ham Green.

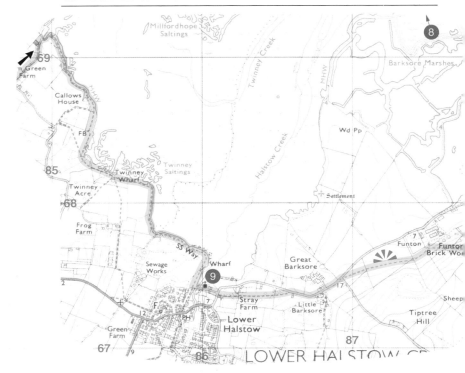

Now go down Shoregate Lane, from where you have views across saltings and creeks and over the Chetney Peninsula, to the Isle of Sheppey. At the end turn right along a farm track, then left over a stile beside the boatyard of the Shoregate Wharf Sailing Club.

You are now beside Halstow Creek. Lying ahead of you, before the Chetney Peninsula, are saltings and the Barksore Marshes, sometimes pronounced 'Basher'. At their point, running into Halstow Creek, is Stangate Creek **8**. Here two hospital ships, lazarettos, used to be stationed for quarantine and for checking imported goods.

Now you turn right and follow the sea wall, ignoring all turnings to the right, for one and a half miles (2.5 km). As you approach Lower Halstow you can see its church right beside the creek **9**. This was a fishing community, then a busy place where barges collected bricks and clay. The church of St Margaret of Antioch was built on the site of a Saxon church. It has superb murals and a Norman font inside. Outside, in the walls, you can see some of the tiles the Romans left behind.

To continue the Shore Way go left along the road past the church to the junction with the Sheerness Road, still the route to the King's Ferry. Cross a stile ahead, just to the right, and walk towards an orchard, then follow waymarking to a stile at the far side before a house. Turn right onto the road, and continue for 400 yards (370 metres) to the next junction. Go diagonally across the road and take the signed route up the field.

No matter how fascinating the marshes are, it is always good to gain height and from here you have a fine view over Halstow Creek and towards the Hoo Peninsula. The surrounding land was owned in the middle ages by the monks of Christ Church, Canterbury, who, good farmers as always, produced plentiful crops of wheat. Later the land became part of the rich North Kent fruit belt, with orchards stretching down to the shoreline. Though some orchards still remain many have been turned to other uses.

Go to the far corner of the field, then continue on the same line across the next field. Cross a farm track, and follow the fence line to the corner of the brickworks. Turn right over a stile, then go left, past the back of the Redland Brick Company to another stile. Now walk diagonally up the hill, past a marker post, to a gate and stile on the far side.

Halstow Creek once teemed with sprit-sail barges laden with mud or bricks.

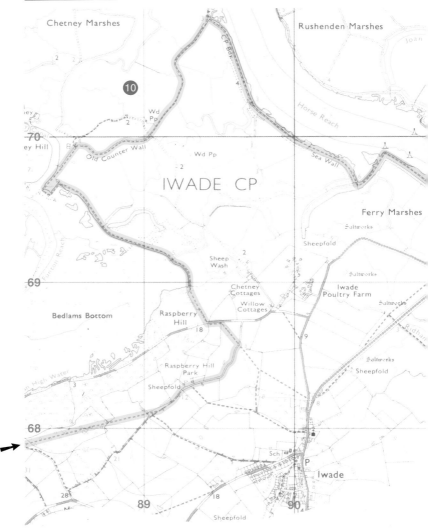

Walk beside a line of pollarded poplars to a farm track. Cross this, pass a ruined shed, then turn right over a stile. Walk across the field to a stile in the middle of the fence. Cross into an old orchard and follow the track to an open field, once orchard. Now head slightly right towards a marker in the old hedge line, and on to the far hedge, one quarter of a mile (400 metres) in all. Go through the hedge to another broad field. From here you can see the cranes of Ridham Dock to the right of the Kingsferry Bridge.

Now make for the far lefthand corner of the field, turn left over a stile and walk past Raspberry Hill Farm. Follow the farm track for about 500 yards (450 metres) and turn left across a field to the road. Go left, leaving the hedge on your right, to the corner of the field. Turn right over a stile, then cross the road and make your way down the slopes of Raspberry Hill towards Chetney Marshes **10**.

Here is yet another marvellous breeding habitat for wildfowl, one of the best in this outstanding area. Avocets and shelduck, pochard and gadwall are all regular visitors.

At a stile set in a line of hawthorns, turn right along the sea wall and continue for half a mile (800 metres) towards a farm. Skirt the small promontory opposite Chetney Hill, then turn right and walk to a gate, before leaving the farm on your left and continuing to the main farm track. Cross and follow the old counter-wall to the Swale. Now turn right and walk beside the Swale towards the Kingsferry Bridge.

In spite of the current sewage problem and traffic to Ridham Dock, Horse Reach is a popular area for watersports since it has one of the few sites with hard landing, beside the bridge. At the Kingsferry **11** a cable-ferry operated for centuries from the mainland to the Isle of Sheppey. So essential was it that local inhabitants had to subscribe to its upkeep. The crossing was free to passengers, except, it seems, on certain feast days, on Sundays and after 8 p.m. The ferryman had the right to free oyster-fishing. A road and rail bridge was first built in 1861, then replaced in 1904. The existing bridge dates from 1961; the span lifts to allow access to Ridham Dock.

Along the next five miles (8 km) to Sittingbourne, past Ridham Dock, beside the Kemsley Marshes and alongside Milton Creek, you pass several factories and meet other strong signs, smells and noises, of industry. You could well choose to take the train from Swale Halt to Sittingbourne but you must flag down the train if you wish it to stop.

If you continue along the Shore Way, you will be rewarded by one of the best views of Elmley Island on the Isle of Sheppey and by another view eastwards, along the Swale to Minster Marshes and Harty. Milton Creek itself is full of interest, both historic and environmental. What is more, the water in the creek has become, in the mid 90s, purer and more oxygenated than in many years. The smell is less strong and life has begun to return to the water. Hasted talked of the 'badness of the water and the gross unwholesomeness of the air'. Things may at last be improving.

To reach the railway station, turn right at the car park and follow the lane up to the road where you will find Swale Halt on the far side of the road to your left.

Otherwise, to follow the Shore Way, continue under the Kingsferry Bridge, turn right onto the sea wall behind the mooring slip, cross a stile tucked into the high wire fence of the Kingsferry Boat Club and walk along the sea wall. Go as far as the navigation pylon **E**, then turn right over a stile. Follow the retaining wall of Ridham Dock to its end, crossing first a road, then a small railway.

Turn left beside a gate and walk beside the road. Where the road swings right you continue across it and walk below Ridham Dock along a cinder track until you come on to the sea wall. Turn

Industry is a constant presence beside the shores of the River Medway.

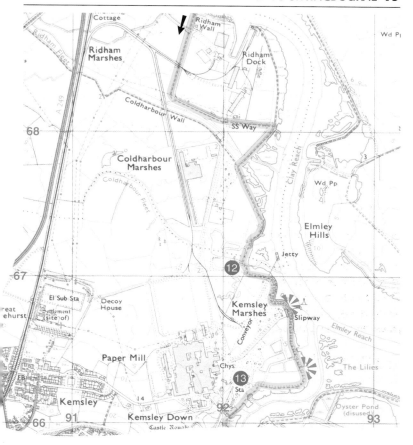

right and walk beside the Swale, past old jetties, long disused, until you come to the cleaning pools of the paper mills **12**. Paper has been made at Kemsley for over 200 years. Today two firms operate here, dealing mainly with recycled paper. Follow the cinder path left, then right, under a conveyor belt. Go between bollards and continue along the sea wall, past the old landfill site to the mouth of Milton Creek.

Where the creek narrows the path now swings right, onto a rubble foundation. At the entrance to works, go down a slope to the left and walk below a fence. You will soon reach more open ground. To your right you now see the station of the Sittingbourne and Kemsley Light Railway **13**, and its steam engines, built for the paper mills at Kemsley.

The Elmley Ferry provided a valuable link between the mainland and the Isle of Sheppey, especially in the days before the Kingsferry Bridge was first built.

Just beyond is the site of Castle Rough **14** where, reputedly, the Danes settled in 893 during one of their raids. They were held back by King Alfred from doing further damage.

From here you continue along the wall for a quarter of a mile (400 metres) until you come to scrub and trees. Leave these to your left **F** and go along the side of a field to a gravel path.

To your right you see Holy Trinity Church, Milton **15**, at Milton Regis, half a mile (800 metres) away at the head of the creek. Milton Regis was one of the oldest settlements in this part of Kent. Trade in corn, fruit and fish flourished from the quays on Milton Creek and it owned oyster beds stretching well out into the Medway.

Turn left at the path, then right, on to higher, reclaimed ground recently planted with trees. Where the trees end you swing right along the edge of meadow, and follow the path to the head of the creek.

At the narrowest point, where you turn sharp right, you see Crown Quay **16** on the far side. Here you may still see sprit-sail barges lined up beside the Dolphin Museum. Soon you see St Michael's church, Sittingbourne **17**, on the skyline. Now go along the creek wall to a narrow path between high wire fences. At the end, turn left into Gas Road **G**, then left again at the main road, Mill Way. Continue at the first roundabout, then swing left to another roundabout which goes into Eurolink Way.

Turn right under the railway bridge, then go left if you want to reach the railway station.

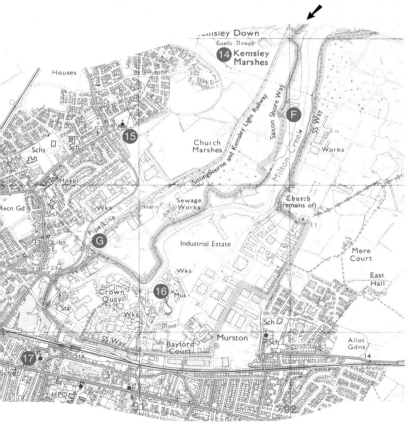

4 BESIDE THE SWALE

Sittingbourne to Faversham   *15¼ miles miles (24.4 km)*

From Sittingbourne the Shore Way now returns to run beside the Swale before exploring the creeks of Conyer, Faversham and Oare. It goes through land which has considerably changed in character over the centuries. Initially it was saltings, later it was reclaimed to form marshland for grazing. In the nineteenth century the area was heavily used for brick-making. Today you see some arable land, but much of the area consists of freshwater grazing marsh, intersected by dykes and fleets. Beside Conyer Creek and Faversham Creek you pass saltmarsh and mudflats. Almost all forms part of the important Swale SSSI, so you can expect some spectacular sights when birds are migrating.

If you are continuing from the previous section of the walk turn left at the roundabout, into Eurolink Way **A** and walk to the next roundabout **B**, then ahead in the next section of Eurolink Way. If you come by train, turn left as you leave the station and walk 500 yards (450 metres), then turn left under the railway into Crown Quay Lane. At the roundabout **B** you turn right. At Crown Quay **1** itself you will find the Dolphin Sailing Barge Museum.

Walk along Eurolink Way, turn left into Castle Road, then, after 500 yards (450 metres), turn right into Dolphin Road. At the top turn left into Church Road and go ahead for 600 yards (540 metres). At the end of the road turn left by the old Murston church **2**. This is the central chancel only of the twelfth-century church. The rest was dismantled and some parts used in the nineteenth-century church **3** in Murston village centre.

Now go down to the edge of the creek **C** where in the nineteenth and early twentieth centuries so many Thames barges were moored that at times it was possible to walk the length of the creek stepping from one to another. The barges took the newly made bricks to London, returning with rubbish to tip and with manure for the orchards.

Turn right **C**, pass the old Brickmakers Arms and walk on until the land opens out. Follow the creek for half a mile (800 metres), then turn left over a stile by the old Oyster Ponds **4**, now a home

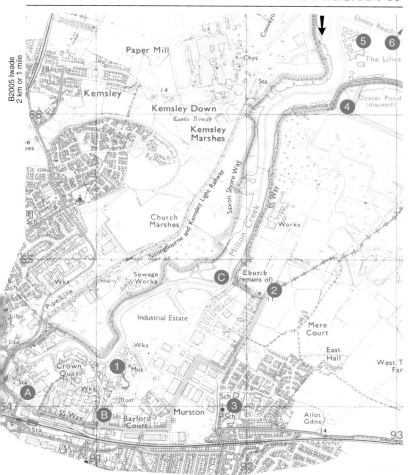

to wildfowl. Here the paper mills dominate the far bank of the creek but the views ahead and to the east are soon open.

Ahead you can see the saltings known as The Lilies **5** and, beyond, Elmley Island on the Isle of Sheppey. Still an island in the early nineteenth century, the Elmley Marshes **6** today form an important nature reserve.

You now walk for two and three-quarter miles (4.5 km) along the sea wall beside the Swale to the mouth of Conyer Creek. Even before the deserted Elmley Ferry you will leave industrialisation behind you and the walk is fresh and relaxed.

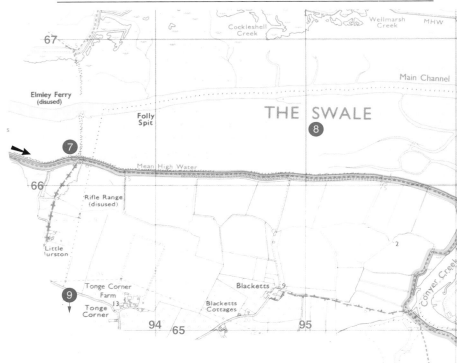

The Elmley Ferry **7**, long disused, enabled local
people to take their horses and cattle to and from
Sheppey. James II tried to flee the country from here in
1688.

The Swale **8**, still occasionally called the River Swale, is
by no means a river, rather a submerged valley. In Roman
times it was probably twice its present width and for centuries ships used it when bound for London from the English
Channel. Boats still sail with reasonable comfort up to an hour
either side of low water. The tide ebbs and flows from both ends
of the channel; the ebb can be fast, sometime up to four knots, but
this varies according to the place. On very high tides the tidal
streams meet somewhere near the mouth of Milton Creek.

To the north, on the Isle of Sheppey, lie the Spitend Marshes, an
important RSPB reserve. From autumn on you will see the skies
here full of migrant birds coming to overwinter, attracted by the
marsh and by the invertebrate-rich mud of the Swale.

On the higher ground to the south lies Tonge **9** where, legend
has it, Vortigern, King of Kent, offered Hengist as much land as he

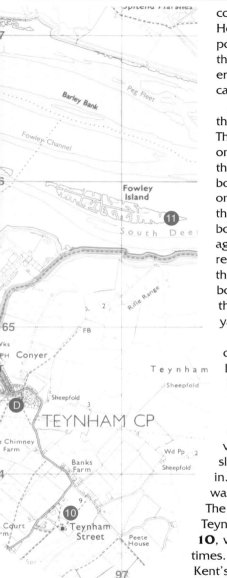

could cover with an ox-hide. Hengist extracted the maximum possible by cutting the hide into thin strips, thongs, which covered enough ground to build a castle.

At the mouth of Conyer Creek the wall and path bend right. The head of the channel seems only to be marked by withies but this is a good haven for small boats. You now walk south for one mile (1.6 km) to the head of the creek. When you reach the boatyards turn half-left then left again and walk on until you reach the road. Turn left **D** along the road, past modern weatherboarded houses. You will find the Ship Inn three hundred yards (270 metres) ahead.

Conyer Creek was once full of barges, taking not only bricks from the nearby works but fruit from local orchards. Immediately to the south the ground has always been rich and fertile. In Roman times vineyards flourished on the slopes and the sea lapped close in. From the eighth century this was part of the Canterbury lands. The archbishops had a palace at Teynham Street, beside the church **10**, where Henry III stayed several times.

Kent's orchards were born here, for it was at Teynham that King Henry VIII's fruiterer first planted carefully imported stock to replace the exhausted fruit trees brought by the Normans centuries before. The whole area from Rainham to Blean became known as the cherry garden and apple orchard of Kent.

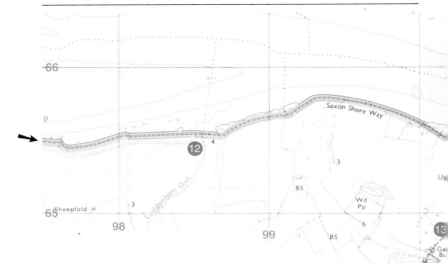

One hundred yards (90 metres) beyond The
Ship take the path ahead and walk, first, alongside
orchards, then across open ground until you reach the sea wall.
Now walk alongside the Swale for two and a half miles (4 km) to
Harty Ferry. You can see a Cardinal buoy marking the east end of the
long shoal at Fowley Island **11**. Now a feeding ground for oyster-
catchers and black-headed gulls, this was once a much longer saltmarsh platform, and home to numerous nesting birds.

The land here remained mainly saltmarsh, with tidal creeks, until
the walls were built after the 1953 floods. Then the marsh gradually
changed to freshwater grazing marsh. The drainage had to be recon-
sidered and the numerous dykes were excavated or developed to
drain excess water from the new farmland. At Luddenham Gut **12**
you pass the main drainage channel for the northern stretch.

The strip of marshland narrows as you skirt the end of the Uplees
Peninsula. You will see a number of small mounds scattered around.
These were used by the explosives works at Uplees **13**. Soon you
enter the KTNC Oare Nature Reserve and then skirt the remains of
the wooden dock used by the explosives works and continue to
Harty Ferry where a road leads down to Oare.

The reserve is now managed to maintain a mosaic of different
types of sward. You will now see, among other birds, teal and gadwall, godwit and whimbrel. In summer reed buntings and sedge
warblers join mallard, coot, shoveler and moorhen to breed in the
dykes. An interesting Interpretation Centre stands at Harty Ferry **14**.

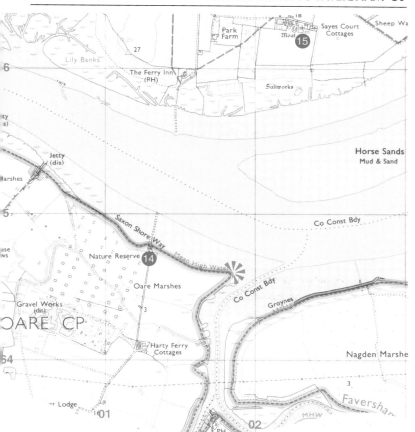

Harty Ferry is a busy centre for sailors, walkers and birdwatchers. In recent years efforts have been made to revive the old ferry to Sheppey but the inshore mud has proved too much. You must be content, for the present, to view the lovely Norman church of St Thomas **15** from a distance.

Continue along the sea wall for one mile (1.6 km) through land which was in the last century still a series of saltings separated by creeks, to the mouth of Faversham Creek. The views are superb here. The shingle spit across the Swale on the Isle of Sheppey stretches out to Shell Ness, Whitstable lies ahead and, in summer, sea lavender clothes the saltings beside you. But, to continue, you swing right to follow the sea wall for one and a half miles (2.4 km) to Oare.

After three-quarters of a mile (1.2 km) the main creek swings eastward and you now follow Oare Creek, a lively place in the sailing season, though at low tide the channel narrows to exclude, seemingly, all but the smallest boats. On the small escarpment to your right stands the church of St Peter, Oare **16**. Its graveyard straggles across the slope.

At the last kissing gate you emerge onto a metalled track by The Castle free house **E**. Here turn left, cross the road bridge, then, just after the Western Link Road on the right, turn left and go

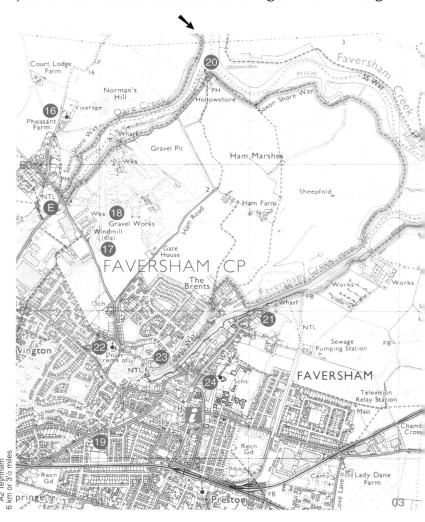

down a metalled track. You pass a lake converted from old workings to your right, a marine yard on left.

Just to the south of the gravel pits stands a tower windmill **17**. To your right are more disused gravel pits, on the site of one of Faversham's gunpowder works **18**. Gunpowder was manufactured at Faversham from the end of the sixteenth century. The government took the works over in 1760 and the marsh sites here opened in 1786. At the Home Works **19** one of the Chart Mills has survived almost intact and has been restored for viewing by the Faversham Society.

At a corrugated barn leave the metalled track as it turns right to a large gate, and turn left along a gravel track following the signstone. Take care for the next 200 yards (180 metres) as the path, really the old sea wall, is loose and crumbling. Continue ahead where a road comes in from the right, passing moored boats beside the creek.

At Hollowshore **20** beside the Shipwright's Arms at the junction of Oare Creek and Faversham Creek turn right and follow the sea wall for two miles (3.2 km) until you come level with moored boats at Faversham's Standard Quay **21**. Here you can see the large brick-built store of the Oyster Company and warehouses, some of them medieval. For much of the way you can see the pinnacles of St Mary's, Faversham on the skyline.

Turn right at a brick wall, follow the path to the end of the works and turn left. Now go along a narrow lane beside houses to a road. Here you pass four brick cottages in the Upper Brents, then turn left and skirt some new weather-boarded buildings to rejoin the edge of the creek. Turn right and continue to another row of cottages in the Front Brents. The Albion pub is on your right with good car parking.

If you turn right when you reach the road you soon come to Stonebridge Pond and the church of St Mary Magdalen, which was once the nave of Davington Priory **22**. Otherwise, to continue along the Way, turn left and cross a swing bridge **23**. Turn left into Conduit Street almost beneath the Shepherd and Neame Brewery, founded in 1698. Here you pass the Sea Cadets' headquarters, a timber-framed warehouse on the Town Quay, first built in 1475 and now named TS *Hazard*, after the ship that Faversham sent to fight against the Armada. Pass The Swan and Harlequin and swing right, up Quay Lane. St Mary's church **24** stands ahead of you, while Abbey Street runs on your left; the main town of Faversham is to your right.

If you turn right into Court Street and continue to the Market Place, you pass some fine seventeenth- and eighteenth-century houses. The sixteenth-century Guildhall stands at the southern end. At this junction you come to Market Street, where, in No 12,

This fifteenth-century timber-framed warehouse at Town Quay which stands at the memory of the ship that Faversham sent to help defeat the Armada.

James II was held a prisoner after local fishermen captured him attempting to escape to France.

Faversham's grew in importance during the middle ages as a port on what was then a large inlet of the Swale and also as a town beside Watling Street, the vital link between Canterbury and London. It first had a charter in Saxon times. Henry II granted another which gave it the right to trade tax-free throughout England. Faversham, as a 'limb' of the Cinque Ports, was virtually

ead of Faversham Creek is now home to sea cadets, and named the TS Hazard, *in*

independent. It was also the town chosen by King Stephen as the site for an abbey that would rival Westminster Abbey and serve as a burial place for himself and his descendants.

Faversham's prosperity grew through shipbuilding and from its gunpowder mills. Its fisheries also played a major role, for the oyster beds to the west of Faversham were among the best along the coast while its Oyster Fishery Company is said to be the oldest in the world. Its breweries still flourish.

5 FROM THE MARSHES TO THE SEA

Faversham to Reculver 18½ miles (29.6 km)

Now you come to the very best of Faversham, Abbey Street, one of the finest old streets in Kent. Its houses are mainly medieval with some eighteenth-century additions. Walk from the junction with Quay Lane and Church Street **A**, along Abbey Street, taking time to look at numbers 82 to 84. Arden Cottage and Arden's House **1** are especially fine, both jettied with good timbers. This was the house of Thomas Arden, mayor in 1547, whose savage murder by his wife became the subject of the Elizabethan play *Arden of Faversham*. To the right lay Faversham's abbey, built by King Stephen in 1147. Arden's House, which was once the guest house, incorporates part of the original gateway.

At the end of Abbey Street turn left by the Anchor Inn, then right along Standard Quay **2**. Go to the right of the Oyster Bay House **3**, then return to the creek and pass the Iron Wharf boatyard. Cross a narrow bridge and go ahead past the sewage works, taking the path along the raised dyke to walk out towards the marshes.

At a junction of tracks **B**, follow the sea wall left round the dyke, turn right down a short slope, cross a stile and make for the lane at the top of field. Here go left to pass Nagden Cottages, from where a small ferry once ran. Turn left at Nagden Farm and cross a field, go along the lefthand side, then turn right onto the sea wall.

Half a mile (800 metres) on from Nagden Farm you cross a stile which marks the edge of the South Swale Nature Reserve **4**. Here you pass reedbeds and saltings specially managed for their wildlife. The pasture is left ungrazed; the reedbeds are cut back from time to time to stimulate new growth; some areas have had topsoil removed to encourage invertebrates and so attract more birds. Here you will see lapwing and redshank or hear the skylark and meadow pipit in season. The drainage dykes below the sea wall are dredged in rotation to maintain a varied range of habitats. Look out for the gatekeeper, Essex skipper and meadow brown butterflies.

As you come round to the head of the creek you will see sea lavender and golden samphire on the saltings. At the shingle bank at Castle Coote **5** you will spot sea kale and sea beet as well as the dramatically named vipers bugloss, dragons' teeth and biting stonecrop.

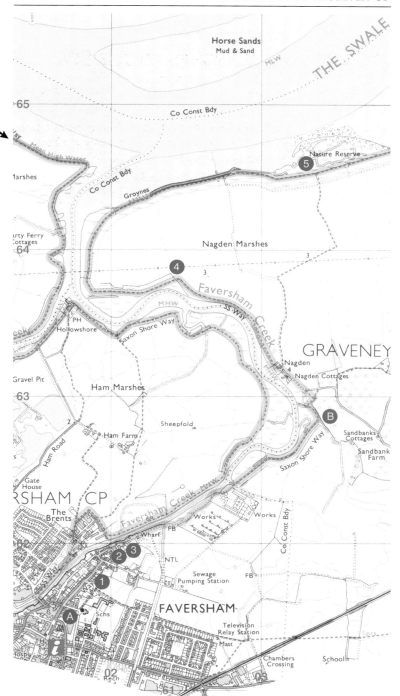

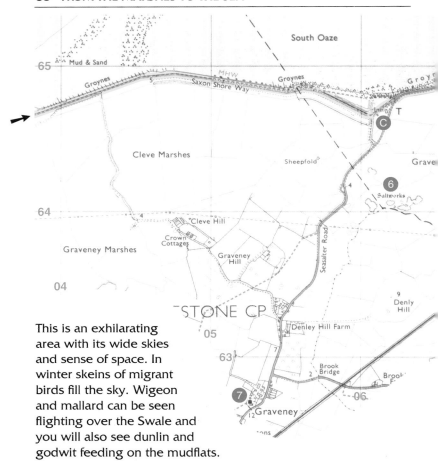

This is an exhilarating area with its wide skies and sense of space. In winter skeins of migrant birds fill the sky. Wigeon and mallard can be seen flighting over the Swale and you will also see dunlin and godwit feeding on the mudflats.

You now walk round the spit for four and a half miles (8 km) until you reach a small hamlet and caravan park opposite Shell Ness on the eastern end of Sheppey. Here **C** you will find Ye Old Sportsman Inn, once a fishermen's house surrounded by huts for tanning the sails. During the Napoleonic Wars local smugglers met French prisoners of war here and led them through the reedbeds to escape to France.

This was once a busy area. Near Ye Old Sportsman you can see mounds which indicate medieval saltworks **6**. In the tenth century the tidal mudflats, creeks and saltings extended almost as far as Graveney itself. In a nearby creek, six feet (2 metres) down, a tenth-century trading vessel was found. The Graveney Boat, is now in the National Maritime Museum, Greenwich. A church, All Saints **7**,

stands beside the old water's edge. It has a Norman chancel and fine, Decorated tracery in the windows. Continue from Ye Old Sportsman, along the new sea wall, above the Faversham Road for half a mile (800 metres). The old sea walls **8**, running south of the road beside the Graveney marshes, were built in the early fourteenth century. You can see a marker **9** indicating the wreck of an old brig, one of many to be wrecked off these shores. After half a mile (800 metres) cross the road and continue along the right-hand side of the road past bungalows and beach huts to the Blue Anchor Corner **D**, another mile (1.6 km) ahead.

Bones washed out of the beach suggest there was an ancient burial site here. By late Anglo-Saxon times Seasalter was a flourishing port, possibly trading with France and perhaps further north, and specialising in the export of salt. Fishing was also an important activity but for home consumption, it seems, as Seasalter was recorded in Domesday Book as a borough belonging to the Archbishop's kitchen. Its oyster beds were carefully conserved.

Cross the road and follow the shoreline past the Seasalter Ski Club, over steps and a stile, walk past houses and continue along the edge of a verge to Admiralty Walk. Turn right over the railway bridge, then go left **E** along the road for about 500 yards (450 metres).

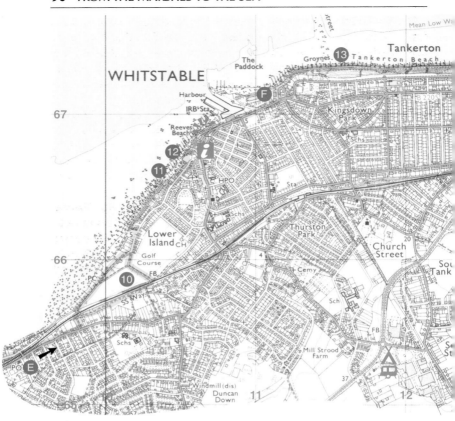

Just past The Rose in Bloom pub turn left, down a narrow path, towards the railway. Here you have a choice of routes. Either go down to the railway line, cross the bridge, turn back along the sea wall and go on to where the concrete changes to a gravel track. Or, just before you reach the railway, turn right and follow a path along the hillside, then cross a railway bridge 500 yards (450 metres) to the east of the first one. Follow a raised dyke across the golf course **10**. The area was once salt pans which used to be flooded at high tide, then allowed to dry out for salt to be collected. Turn right and join the gravel track 150 yards (140 metres) ahead.

At a weatherboarded house, No 122, turn left to the seafront, then right, up steps, and make for Whitstable along the the shore until you reach The Old Neptune **11**. Much battered by storm and flood, this has been an ale-house for two hundred years. Before that it was a fisherman's cottage.

At Whitstable the coastline was, in Roman times, almost a mile further out. Storm and tide eroded it and the fact that the town still stands today is thanks largely to its sea walls and sluices. The idea for these was first proposed in 1494. Middle Wall was built in 1583, Island Wall between 1798 and 1806. Sea Wall and the far end of Harbour Street served the same purpose.

The old Horsebridge, the slipway from which horses could walk straight on to a barge, has been reconstructed, the old alleys which connect the walls and the old boatyards converted, but you can still get a feeling of the times when Whitstable provided an anchorage, and when shipbuilders, repairers, sailmakers and chandlers flourished.

From the Old Neptune, turn right for a few yards along Marine Gap, then left to continue along the sea front. You will soon pass *The Old Favourite* **12**, a salvaged yawl first built in 1890 for oyster fishing. Now turn right, along one of the smaller lanes which give access to Island Wall, not Squeezegut Alley, you may be relieved to know, but Collars Alley, then go left along Island Wall. Opposite is Beach Alley, nineteenth-century home of the Ganns, best-known of divers in a town once famous for its diving expertise. Return to the shore at Keam's Yard, an attractive parking place on the site of one of the busiest shipyards. Peter Cushing, the actor, gave his name to the sea wall, one of the places from which in midsummer you can watch the sun set in the east over the Isle of Sheppey.

Turn right along the shore, then right again past the Royal Native Oyster Stores. This was built in 1898 to store oysters for the London market and named after the delicious oysters cultivated here. The Whitstable oyster beds extended over a large area and were renowned for the delicacy of the oysters and for the whiteness of their shells. To this day the annual Oyster Feast is still celebrated in September.

Turn left along sea wall. Continue along Harbour Street for 500 yards (450 metres), passing the harbour entrance on the way. The Canterbury and Whitstable Railway, popularly known as the 'Crab and Winkle Line', was opened in May, 1830, the first train being pulled by 'Invicta'. It was the first line ever to operate fully under steam power. The harbour was built in 1832, to import coal and link with the railway. Today the harbour shelters a small inshore fishing fleet.

Just beyond a swimming pool and bowling alley turn left **F** down Beach Walk, then right, onto the Tankerton Promenade **13**.

In the seventeenth and eighteenth centuries the mineral copperas, collected from the shore, was treated to give crystals used in cloth-dying, causing an acrid smell of sulphur to permeate the air. Now sulphur is found in name only, in sulphur weed, the rare hog's fennel, which grows on the slopes and is host to the equally rare moth *Agonopterix putridella*.

You see commercial vessels on the horizon as they make up the Princes Channel for the Thames. The permanent structures rising out to sea are the Maunsell Sea Forts at Shivering Sands and Red Sands, built in 1943 to help combat German aircraft. Soon you can see the landing stage at Herne Bay, all that now remains of the pier.

After three miles (5 km) you reach a slipway used for water sports at Hampton Lane **G**. Here follow the sea wall to the left past a play area, go up to the Hampton Pier **14** beside the Hampton Inn, then turn right and walk, first below, then along, the Western Esplanade, which becomes the Central Parade at Herne Bay.

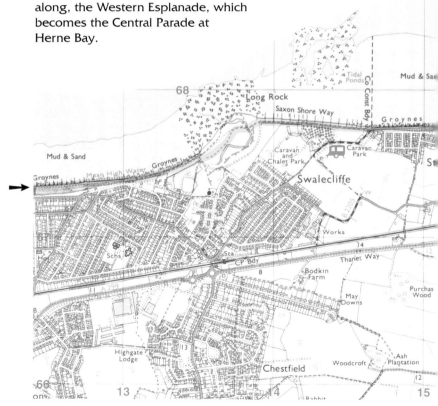

Herne Bay grew up in the nineteenth century as a seaside resort. The pier **15** was destroyed in a storm in 1979. The Clock Tower **16**, built for the coronation in 1837, shows the classical spirit with its Doric and Corinthian columns. Towards the end of the parade you can see some attractive terrace houses with bow windows from the 1830s.

Where the Central Parade turns right into Canterbury Road **H**, go ahead along the East Cliff Parade, past the Kings Hall Theatre and along the undercliff. If you prefer to walk on a softer surface or if the tide is high and the wind strong you may take the track on the other side of the sea wall along the rough ground of The Downs or Beltinge Cliff.

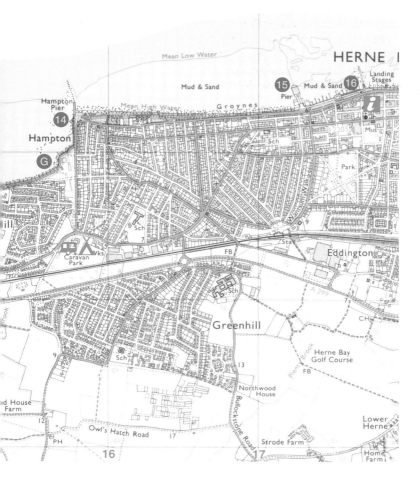

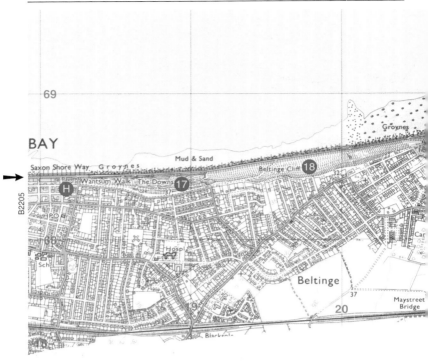

A beacon on the slopes above the Downs **17** relayed news of the Armada to the Isle of Sheppey. Ahead you will see the ruins of the church at Reculver.

For the next two and a half miles (4 km), between the Downs and Reculver, stretch cliffs formed from the sandstones and clays laid down some 60 million years ago. These rocks contain numerous fossil plants which make this an especially rich area for geological research. Different approaches to sea defence have had interesting effects. At Beltinge **18** the sea wall has saved the soft London clay from further erosion. This has created a slope now colonised by grasses and wildflowers which are hosts to many butterflies, such as the red admiral and the painted lady. At Bishopstone Glen **19** the sea still scours the undercliff and you can see the clay beds, lower London Tertiary layers, which were deposited above the chalk. You can see the entire succession if you walk along the shore below the cliffs

At the end of the promenade follow the road uphill, then skirt the car park, by the Bay Sea View Rest Home, and descend to

369820 5 Landon Rd.

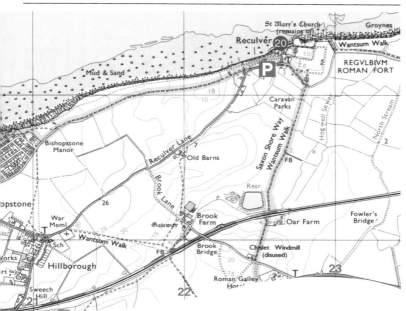

Bishopstone Glen and the Reculver Country Park. Cross a bridge over the Glen, and follow the path back to the edge of the cliff. Turn right where steps go left down to the beach. The riot of hawthorn and sweet briar you see in early summer offers a home to an important colony of sandmartins.

Continue to a field where you see the coastguard house ahead just beyond a thick hedge. Make for the far righthand corner. Here, at the end of Bishopstone Lane, take the broad, grassy path which leads for one mile (1.6 km) down to Reculver. Over on your right you can see the towers, three in all, of Richborough Power Station which will dominate the skyline for the next ten miles (16 km). Ahead, beyond the low ground of the Wade Marsh where the Wantsum Channel once flowed, rises the Isle of Thanet. Swing left when you reach the end of the grassy track, go onto a concrete path and continue to the Interpretation Centre. If you want to know more of the area's history, geology and wildlife, this is the place to visit.

The towers at Reculver **20**, known to mariners as 'The Reculvers', were spared demolition at the request of Trinity House and provide an important navigation mark. They are a stark testimony to the long history of this site, now only preserved from

The twin towers of the ruined church of St Mary at Reculver mark the site of the Saxo

destruction by the sea defences. Here, on a peninsula stretching three-quarters of a mile (1.2 km) northwards, Iron-Age Celts had a settlement. Later, the Romans built a fort and, later still, the Saxons established a church.

Regulbium was first fortified in the first century AD soon after *Rutupiae*, at Richborough, and was then developed in the third and fourth centuries as part of the Saxon Shore defences. The name of the nearby pub recalls the next stage, for King Ethelbert who welcomed St Augustine to the Saxon coast ruled, some say,

re fort of Regulbium *and of one of the country's earliest churches.*

from here. His successor, Egbert, built the Saxon church and monastery. The Normans rebuilt the church and dedicated it to St Mary. The building which had survived so much was finally all but demolished in 1801 when it was removed to nearby Hillborough. So much has been washed away that it is difficult to tell exactly what was there but today you can still see the outline of some of the original buildings on the ground.

One thing remains, Alexanders, the spring cabbage imported by the Romans and now growing around the towers.

6 THE OLD SHORELINE

Reculver to Deal

20½ miles (32.8 km)

The route now takes you along the shoreline of the old Wantsum Channel which once separated the mainland of Kent from the Isle of Thanet. You pass through the quiet, open agricultural land of East Kent, much of it created as land was reclaimed in medieval times. You hear the sound of the curlew, see lapwing and golden plover in the fields and hear the skylark in summer. The dykes are lined with yellow iris and meadowsweet. Beside the old drove roads whitethroat and willow warbler join numerous other birds at nesting time.

From Grove Ferry you follow the Little Stour, then the Great Stour, tidal all your way. You go beside the Ash Levels with their intricate system of drainage, walls and counter- walls. Names here – Abbot's Wall, Monkton and Monk's Wall – recall the people who helped to create this landscape in the post-Norman days. Then you reach the second and largest of the Saxon Shore Forts, *Rutupiae*, at Richborough. From there you come to the Cinque Port of Sandwich, then walk on to the fishing port of Deal.

Leaving Reculver, pass the Information Office on your right, then take the path which runs diagonally across the sports area. Follow the sign along the rough track between the caravan stores on your right and the caravan park on your left until you come to a broad dyke immediately after a hedge, at the beginning of open fields.

Turn right between the supports of the power lines and follow the dyke along a grassy path. You now strike inland across reclaimed marshland making for rising ground and trees and walking along a path through cultivated land beside a broad dyke. As you follow its curve you see the railway line ahead. Half a mile (800 metres) on, turn right onto a concrete farm track, then turn immediately left under the railway and continue uphill towards the road, past kennels.

You now leave Chislet mill to your right **1**. What you see here is the octagonal base from a smock mill, the last of a line which stood on this site from the thirteenth century onwards. This one, built in 1765, was destroyed by sudden storm in 1916.

Turn left at the top **A**, then immediately right, following the road sign to Chislet and Upstreet. The road below you was built in

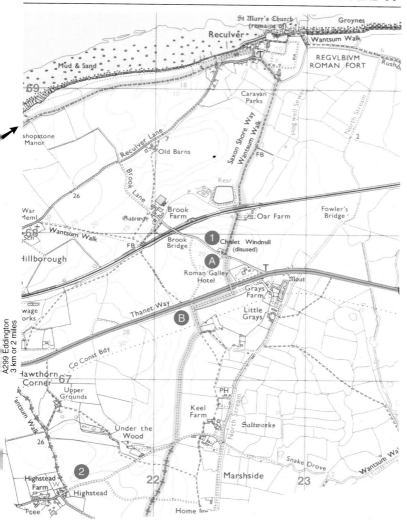

1934. The Roman Galley Inn, built at the same time, can be reached by going ahead from **A**, almost to the junction with the A299. Turn left **B** and follow a metalled lane for half a mile (800 metres) to a cross-roads.

You now follow a quiet lane, with fine views over the long-reclaimed marshland. The slopes to your right at Highstead **2** were once occupied by the Beaker people from Northern Europe around 2,000 BC. At 90 feet, (30 metres) above sea level Highstead was later the obvious place in this area to site a beacon to signal the news of the Armada across the low ground to Thanet.

The Wantsum Channel **3** once came within one quarter of a mile (400 metres) of the path. It was already silting up in Roman times and the Chislet Marshes were 'inned', then reclaimed, in the twelfth and thirteenth century by the Augustinian monks from Canterbury based at Chislet. You can see remains of saltworks **4** – Domesday Book claims there were 47 in the area – just beyond the old drove road which runs beside the marsh. Almost a mile (1.6 km) beyond you can see the sea wall beside the Whitfield Sewer **5**, built to protect the area from high tides.

Above Keel Farm, cross the road and take the lane ahead, continuing along the old road along the marshes, known as the Port Way. Ahead, where you see the triple oasts and Dutch gable, lies Chislet **6**, one of the oldest and largest manors belonging to St Augustine's Abbey. After half a mile (800 metres) turn left down a field at the second of two houses. At the bottom turn right before the hedge, pass a half-hipped weatherboarded barn and two thatched cottages, then, after a series of stiles, turn left towards the road.

Cross and go along a small track past a Wesleyan chapel, cross the road and go down a narrow lane to the left of a white-painted house. Cross a stock-proof bridge over the North Stream into an open field. Cross another stock-proof bridge after 200 yards (180 metres), then go right towards the road and turn left along an old drove road, now metalled.

To your left runs Tipper Drove another of the many drove roads which intersected the marshland from late medieval times onwards. Continue in beautiful, unspoilt country to the hamlet of Chitty. Turn right at Lower Chitty Farm, then follow the sign to Upstreet and Sarre along a broad track between high hedges.

Cross the Sarre Penn **C** and turn right beside it, then, where the Sarre Penn bends right, turn left across a cultivated field. Ahead you see a steep bank. Turn right below it, then, almost immediately, follow the sign up the bank, reaching steps as you climb higher. Turn right at the top, skirt the edge of the field for about 250 yards (220 metres), then go left, under power lines, across the field to the road.

You are now beside the A28 Canterbury to Margate road. When first built by the Romans this road ran to the edge of the Wantsum Channel. In medieval times it was extended along the Sarre Wall **7**, built over what was by then swamp and marsh, to reach Sarre, then a flourishing port, and Minster.

Grays

Keel
Farm

PH

North Stream

Saltworks

4

3

River Wantsum

Co Const & CP Bdy

5

Saltworks

der the
Wood

Snake Drove

Wantsum Walk

Whitfield Sewer

Marshside

May Drove

Home
Farm

21

Marshside
Farm

Boyden Gate

Chislet Marshes

2

en-Gate
arm

PH

FB

Gilling Drove (Track)

Marly Pits
(dis)

W

Church Lane

Chitty

Chitty
Farm

CHISLET CP

PH

16

Chitty Lane

Sarre Penn

2

Chislet

6

Sch

C

slet
stal

T

Hollow Street

Sewage
Works

Wantsum Walk

Chislet
South Level

Saxon Shore Way

Wantsum Walk

Walmers
Hill

Saltworks

Wall End

7

Nethergong Penn

Fairfields

Island Road

13

Nethergong
Farm

MS

Upstreet
Farm

3

Co C

Upstreet

22

PO

21

PH

23

Grove
Ferry

PH

24

Grea

10 km or 6 miles
A28 Canterbury

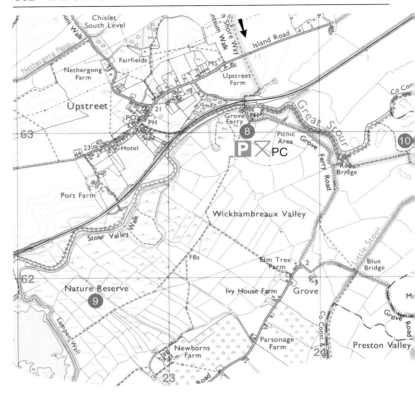

Cross the road, take the path indicated by the fingerpost and head down the slope towards trees. Go down some steps to the road at Grove Ferry **8** on the River Stour, then turn left over the bridge past the Grove Ferry Inn. To the south-east lies the Stodmarsh valley **9**, another area drained by the Augustinian monks. Here they grazed mares in foal, hence the name Stud-marsh. The land is now a National Nature Reserve, famous for its birdlife.

Follow the road round the Inn for 400 yards (360 metres), then turn left into the Grove Ferry picnic site. Turn right and walk along the embankment beside the river for half a mile (800 metres), then drop down as you approach the building at Red Bridge, skirt the side of the field, turn left through a gate and left again. Cross the entrance to the Boat House and turn left over a stile.

Follow the farm track to a derelict barn, then swing left and continue alongside a hawthorn hedge beside a dyke until you reach a gate. To your left you see the ox-bow formation of an earlier line of

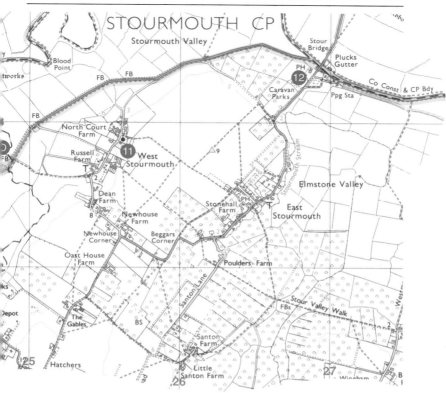

the river **10**. Cross the turf bridge where the ox-bow meets the path. Turn right, then left at a marker post and walk for 100 yards (90 metres) beside the Little Stour.

At **D** turn right over a narrow footbridge, then go left along the east side of the river. Ahead you see West Stourmouth **11**, where the River Stour once entered the Wantsum Channel. Walk on for 250 yards (220 metres), skirt the pumping station and continue along the river's edge for just over a mile (1.6 km). At the end of a line of poplars which acts as a windbreak to orchards, go through a swing gate, passing a caravan site, along a grassy track

Here at Plucks Gutter **12** the Great Stour meets the Little Stour. Just to the south of the path you will find the Dog and Duck, the last pub on the Shore Way before Sandwich.

The path now goes under the bridge and crosses a narrow footbridge over a small dyke, to continue beside the river. Ignore the broad track which runs below the riverbank, being sure to keep to

Hawthorn and cow parsley line the banks of the Little Stour in spring as it flows to jo

e Great Stour near West Stourmouth.

the path beside the river. Follow this for three miles (5 km), over footbridges and a stile, to the railway bridge by Richborough power station **E**.

The River Stour was once tidal up as far as Canterbury. As the Wantsum Channel silted up, so to some extent did the Stour, and Fordwich, one and a half miles (2.5 km) downstream from Canterbury, became the port. In the middle ages stone was the main commodity carried up the river, then coal until the railway from Whitstable and the new harbour there removed the need.

The Stour forms the parish boundary. To the south lies the parish of Ash. The ground rises from the Ash Levels which Hasted dismissed, in his customary way, as 'very wet and unwholesome', to rich and fertile ground further south. The area has a number of fine medieval houses. On the other side of the river you see the raised dyke of the Abbot's Wall **13**, and beyond that, on the Thanet slope, and part of the Christ Church estates, the Monkton Marshes **14** and Monkton church **15**. Soon you see the Norman tower and spire of Minster church **16**, built on a Saxon site. Here the monks of St Augustine's were responsible as they were, too, for the abbey which stands nearby. Ebbsfleet where St Augustine, their founder, landed in 597 **17** is two miles (3.2 km) to the east. Once you are level with Minster you see the walls of the Roman Fort of Richborough at 45 degrees to your right. Ahead lie the power station at Richborough and the wind turbine beside it **18**.

Follow the path under the railway bridge **E**, and then right, with the distinctive swishing sound of the turbine in your ears. Cross a

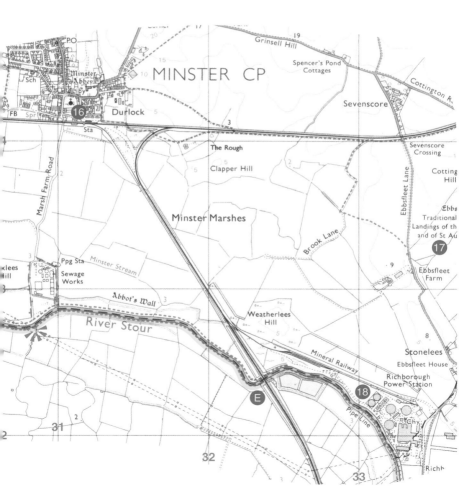

series of stiles and pass under a pipeline. Walk on until you reach a small flight of steps. Turn right up them and walk along raised ground some fifteen feet (3 metres) from the river.

This area, currently being reclaimed, was for a long time an important site for wildfowling. Soon you pass the Stonar Cut **19** which links two points of the River Stour. Over the centuries the drift of sand and shingle from the North Sea, which caused the gradual silting-up of the Wantsum Channel, also created a shingle bank running south from Ebbsfleet. This diverted the mouth of the Stour southwards. Later sand accumulated north of Sandwich and so caused the curious U-bend beside part of which you now walk. The Stonar Cut was made in 1776 across the neck of the bend, to help to drain floodwater which had been pent up as a result of the bend.

Continue past an industrial estate which lies on the other side of the river. Aim for the left of a derelict barn, opposite the Monk's Wall **20** on the other side of the river, and make for a stile just beyond trees. Cross and make your way round the bends in the river and beneath the walls of the Roman fort **21**, the first defence work established by the Romans and later one of their Saxon Shore Forts. You can take a path up the slope **F** to reach the entrance, the museum and the remains of the fortress.

The site, once an island, is impressive. Here, on the edge of the open sea, the Romans established a settlement constructed according to their customary grid plan with roads, barracks and workshops. Soon a flourishing small town grew up with a triumphal arch in the centre which gave a symbolic flourish to this, the port of entry to the province of Britannia. Only later, under threat from the Germanic tribes, were the fortifications developed with the construction of the walls and ramparts whose traces you see today. Sadly the harbour at the gates, which imported the best wine in the Roman world and exported the finest oysters known, was entirely washed away. A museum helps to explain the history.

To continue the Shore Way **F** walk down a grassy track beside the railway. Go beneath the A256 and join the Richborough Road.

Turn left and walk for half a mile to the A257 and the edge of Sandwich **G** from where you can see the Flemish crow-stepped gables of Manwood Court **22**. An eighteenth-century smock windmill lies along the road to the right **23**.

Sandwich, the town on a spit of sand, grew up in the seventh century, becoming important as a gateway to Europe. At the time of Domesday Book it belonged to the Archbishop of Canterbury but already gave ship service to the king. Its prestige reached a peak in the early thirteenth century. The French sacked the town in an attempt to bring help to King John. After John's death in 1217 the boy king, Henry III, defeated the French in the Battle of Sandwich, a fierce sea battle in Pegwell Bay. The Portsmen of Sandwich received generous rewards, and there was enough money left over to found a chapel and hospital dedicated to St Bartholemew on whose day the battle had been won.

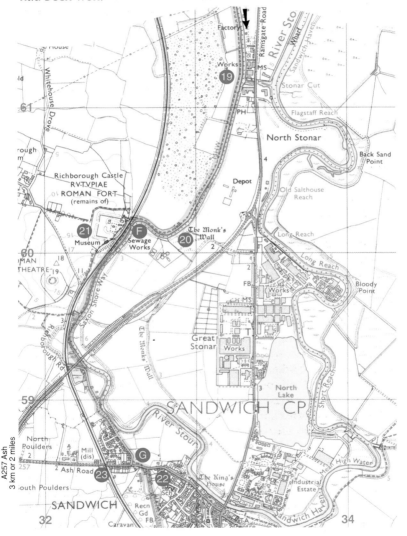

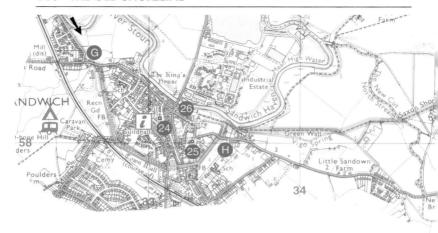

From then on trade flourished, especially in the export of wool. In 1227 Henry III granted a licence for St Clement's Fair which brought considerable prosperity to the town.

Although the harbour later silted up, a new lease of life came with the arrival of the French Huguenots and Flemish protestants in the sixteenth century. Architecture, too, benefited with the arrival of the Dutch gable.

Turn left **G**, then, after 200 yards (180 metres), turn right along The Butts to follow the line of the old town wall of medieval Sandwich. This is a delightful stretch, with meadows to your right beside what is effectively the old moat. You can see the brick tower and cupola of St Peter's church **24** ahead to your left. Cross the Woodnesborough Road, continue along Rope Walk, then Newgate, and finally Mill Wall which has a slight upward incline.

From the highest point of Mill Wall you can see the Norman tower of St Clement's church **25**. Continue to **H**, cross the road 500 yards (450 metres) to the east of the harbour **26** and the Barbican gate, turn right, then, almost immediately, left to cross open space, then turn right where the Vigo Spring meets the Stour. You then cross a small bridge and walk along a metalled path, Green Wall, with reclaimed marshland to your left. After about half a mile (800 metres) take the left fork and in three-quarters of a mile (1.2 km) you reach a gate onto the Royal St George's Golf Links **27**. This famous golf course, frequently host to the Open Championship, was created when the club was founded in 1887.

The path across the links makes for pleasant walking, well-signed and with good links turf underfoot. Between the 5th hole

oyal St George's Golf Links

VORTH CP

27

Old Haven

Toll Gate

Guilford Road

Sandwich Bay Estate

Princes Drive

PCs

Groyne

Old Downs Farm

Ppg Sta

Slipway
Groyne

Dickson's Corner

Downs
dge

e of Dogs

North Stream

Lyddcourt Stile

Lydden

Mary Bax's Stone

Saxon Shore Way

Groynes

Dam & FB

Roaring Gutter

Lydden Valley

Old North Stream

Caravan Park

FB

Pillbox

Royal Cinque Ports Golf Links

Mean Low Water

Mean High Water

36

FB

55

Blackhorse Wall

37

Tenants

and the 6th tee, turn right
onto Princes Drive and walk for
two and a half miles (4 km) to Deal,
passing the Sandwich Bay Estate and
the Royal Cinque Ports Golf Club on your way.

The Barbican in Sandwich, built during the reign of Henry VIII, marks the official entrance to a town which has many reminders of still earlier days.

Sandwich Bay stretches to your left, Pegwell Bay lies behind you with the Thanet cliffs rising up at Ramsgate. The shoreline from here northwards is gradually silting up and today is an important area of unimproved sand dunes, mudflats, saltmarsh and dune pasture. You will find the rare flora associated with such land, including sea holly and yellow rattle. It is an important over-wintering area for migrant birds.

As you approach the houses at the northern end of Deal you pass the site of Sandown Castle **28**. This was the first of the three castles established in the area by Henry VIII in 1539. Its quatrefoil design was repeated in Walmer Castle south of Deal. You then walk along The Marina, the Central Parade and Beach Street until you come to the Pier.

Caravan Site

Walnut Tree Farm

Sandhills

Redhouse

CH

Golf Road

Wall

Hills

BS

28 Sandown Castle (rems of)

BS

Kennels Farm

Allot Gdns

Northwall Road

Sandfield Farm

Groynes

CG Sta

FB

South Wall

FB

Sch

i
PO

Pier

Wks

St

Sch

DEAL

Middle Deal

Hospl

Deal Castle

Bks

Sch

Barracks

LB & IRB Sta

Sch Cemy

Allot Gdns

Walmer Lower Barracks

Saxon Shore Way

Pits (dis)

Sch

Sch

Recn Gd

Walmer

Upper Walmer

A258 Sandwich
7 km or 4½ miles

THE WHITE CLIFFS AND THE CHANNEL

Deal to Crete Road East   *14¾ miles (23.6 km)*

The next section of the walk takes you along some of the most exciting and evocative stretches of all. Soon you see the chalk cliffs rising sheer ahead. Later as you near Folkestone, the cliffs change character but are no less dramatic. All the way you may relive the more than 6,000 years of history that have left their mark on the Channel coast.

Deal's position beside the Downs, the safe anchorage between the land and the notorious Goodwin Sands, always gave it a livelihood as a fishing centre, and fishing boats still rest between tides, drawn up on the beach. The town has also played its part in England's defence. Deal Castle, the largest of all Henry VIII's castles, was built, along with its neighbours at Sandown and Walmer, in 1539-40. From the time of Elizabeth I a naval force was stationed in the Downs and from the seventeenth century a Navy Yard brought trade to the town, fitting-out and supplying the fleet. At about the same time a new town developed away from the fishing huts by the beach. Middle Street **1**, and the alleys around it, are well worth exploring. In them you will see some well-preserved domestic buildings dating from the seventeenth to the nineteenth centuries.

Leave Deal Pier **A** and walk almost due south along the promenade, passing the fishing boats which still line the shore at low tide. Soon you pass the Time–Ball Tower **2**, built as a semaphore station in 1812, then converted in 1855 to use a time-ball, a copper ball raised or dropped at specific times of the day to give Greenwich Mean Time to the ships anchored in the Downs.

Deal has been the base for the Royal Marines since 1861. Beyond the Castle **3**, in the Wellington Parade, you can see the Depot's buildings some of which date from Napoleonic times and which had previously been a military hospital **4**. A memorial bandstand stands on The Green **5**.

After one mile (1.6 km) turn right, then left, along a metalled path, Wellington Parade, past Walmer Castle **6**, where you can see the deep-set gun ports pointing out to sea. The castle was converted for domestic used in the eighteenth century. Today it is the

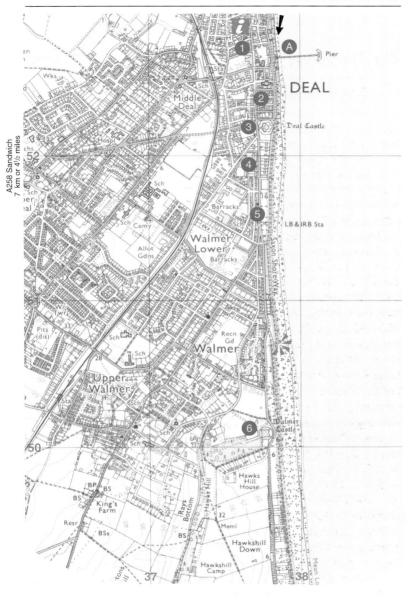

official residence of the Lord Warden of the Cinque Ports and you may see the flag flying if the Queen Mother, Lord Warden since 1979, is in residence.

You now continue for another mile (1.6 km), until you reach the Zetland Arms at Kingsdown **B**. This was long a flourishing community which provided fish in great quantities for markets in London and elsewhere. It was also a strong centre for smuggling. With the Goodwin Sands nearby, the lifeboat based here from 1866 to 1927 saw active times. The rescue of the *Sorrento* in 1872 created one of the legends of lifeboat history.

After the Zetland Arms your next goal is the cliffs which rise ahead. To reach them, turn right immediately, then go left along Undercliffe Road. At the end follow the path up steps to the top of the cliffs. Soon you can see the cliffs north of Pegwell Bay beside Ramsgate, the North Foreland and the Downs, and on a clear day, the cliffs of the French coast as well.

As you walk on, now beside the Walmer and Kingsdown Golf Course, the path is broad and easy, soft turf with patches of chalk showing through. In July you will find *lathyrus* growing wild.

Deal Castle, designed to protect Henry VIII's fleet anchored in the Downs, hugs the ground within its moat.

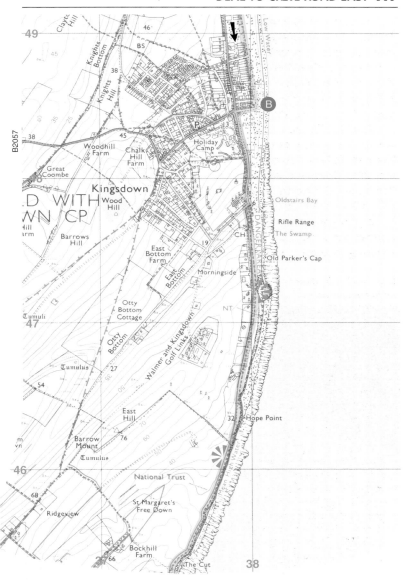

At the end of the golf course, you go through a gate onto the National Trust property of Bockhill Farm. Rolling, cultivated downland stretches to your right; to your left gorse, guelder rose and sweet briar separate you from the cliff edge.

There is now a gentle climb uphill for half a mile (800 metres). When you have almost reached the top, take the left turn **C** at a junction of tracks and go to the seaward side of the old coastguard station. If you prefer you can go ahead at **C**, past the memorial to the Dover Patrol **7**. In this case, to rejoin the Shore Way, turn left from the road at The Leas **D**, then turn right and descend some steep steps to the beach. As an alternative you may stay on the road and rejoin the Way at **E**.

Whichever route you take, it is worth turning up to the village of St Margaret's at Cliffe to see the fine Norman church of St Margaret of Antioch **8**. The Cliff Tavern almost opposite also justifies the detour.It is easy to see why the small bay at St Margaret's **9**, well protected from southerly winds by the towering cliffs,

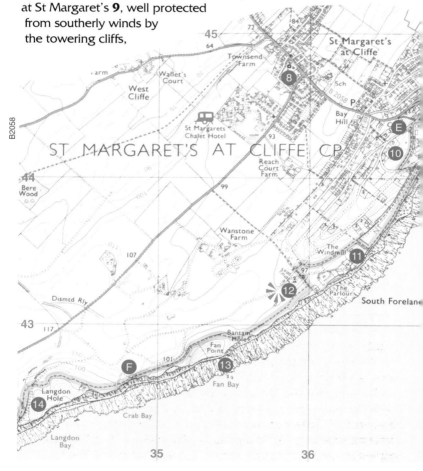

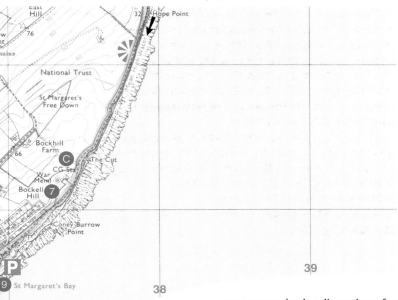

was a regular landing place for smugglers. Today it attracts summer visitors but still keeps its air of seclusion. You can find food and drink at a beach hut, while the Coastguard Inn lies beside the road leading out of the bay. To leave the bay, walk up the road to **E**, then go ahead along the public footpath signed to the Dover Cliff Walk. After 50 yards (45 metres) turn left along Beach Road. Here you will find a museum on the left and the Pines Garden **10** on your right.

At the cross-tracks at the end of the Pines Garden turn left, then right to follow a grassy track along Lighthouse Down. Turn right after 700 yards (630 metres) and rejoin the gravel track just before woodland. The smock windmill **11**, the last to be built in Kent, was erected in 1928 to generate electricity.

After 500 yards (450 metres) follow the waymark left, then left again at the lighthouse **12**. A lighthouse was first erected here in 1634 after a petition by shipowners distressed at the loss of life on the Goodwin Sands. It can be visited during National Trust hours.

Turn right at the cliff and follow a clear path along the cliff top with Dover Harbour within your sight. The headland which rears up beyond is Shakespeare Cliff. Here the steep-sided hollows run down to Fan Bay **13**. At a grassy wall running inland **F**, ignore the right turn and take the signed path round Langdon Hole **14**.

The chalk cliffs at the South Foreland, towering 300 feet above the sea, are the epitor

'The White Cliffs of Dover'.

On the far side of Langdon Hole, you join a tarmac road and walk on past the National Trust viewing area, tea room and car park below Fox Hill Down.

Dover has always provided a haven for shipping. The early harbour lay well within the deep cleft between the two hills but by Saxon times that had silted up. The present harbour was begun in the nineteenth century when successive breakwaters were built which gave protection and stopped the eastward drift of shingle.

Ahead you see Dover Castle **15**, whose stone walls and towers were first built by the Normans but which contains a history far older. Dover's two hills overlooking the Straits had always been a natural place for defence and look-out and Castle Hill was first occupied in the Iron Age. The Romans placed a Pharos, or lighthouse, here in the first century, matching it with another on the Western Heights. The base for their *Classis Britannia*, on top of which the Saxon Shore fort was probably built, was situated in the valley below. Later the Saxons established a fortified town with a church, St Mary-in-Castro, in the centre.

When you reach a hairpin bend, go straight ahead, down steps to a concrete path beneath Jubilee Way. Walk along Atholl Terrace, then below the East Cliff. Turn right onto the main road, Marine Parade, walk along for about 80 yards (75 metres), then cross the A20, following the sign to the sea front.

Turn right into New Bridge **G**, past the memorial to the fallen in the Indian Mutiny, take the underpass beneath Town Wall Street and re-emerge into Bench Street where you will find both pubs and eating

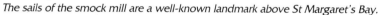

The sails of the smock mill are a well-known landmark above St Margaret's Bay.

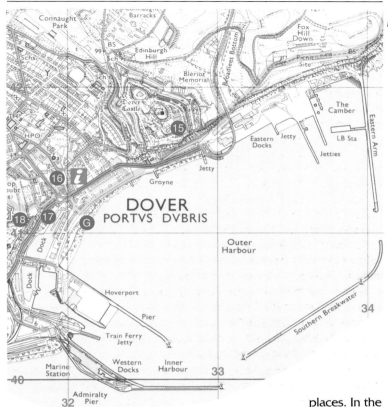

places. In the
Market Square **16** you
will also find signs to all the places of interest, such as the
Roman Painted House which contains part of the Shore fort wall.
Turn left along Queen Street where the Saxon Shore Way joins
the North Downs Way. Cross York Street and turn left, then right,
into Adrian Street. Turn right beneath allotments **17**, once the site
for the Dover Pilots' look-out. Here too, reputedly, stood the
house where Dickens's David Copperfield visited Betsy Trotwood.
Turn left up St Martin's steps, built in Victorian times for visitors to
reach the Heights. It takes 64 steps to reach the slopes above, but
the view from the top is worth the effort. This route used to be the
old road to Folkestone and passed through common grazing land.
Today you will find orchids on the slopes.

At the top go through a kissing gate and up some steps set in
the hillside. Here you see part of the huge structure known as the
Western Heights **18**. When war had been declared with France in

1793 and it was feared that Napoleon would invade, small earthworks already in existence were enlarged to fortify this hill. Work was stopped after Napoleon's defeat and only completed in 1853, when new threats from France arose, to create one of the most complex networks of fortifications in the country.

Skirt the Redoubt and follow the path round the fortifications. Go on to a kissing gate, down some steps onto the North Military Road and turn left down the road, towards St Martin's Battery. Where the road begins to go downhill a viewing area **H** gives a panoramic view of Dover Harbour. At the junction opposite, turn right from the Military Road into Citadel Road. Here you pass the site of a church of the Knights Templar **19**, with its characteristic circular nave, built in 1128.

Just after this fork left, then left again, taking the bridle path downhill. When you come to the corner of the old prison buildings, now an HM Young Offenders Institution, fork left again along a footpath to the brow of the hill. Shakespeare Cliff rises up on the far side of the A20 trunk road.

Follow the path at an angle down the hillside, turn left by the children's play area and go down concrete steps to the top of Ropewalk. Now follow King Lear's Way round, turn left and go along the underpass.

Turn right **I**, then go left up a lane which leads you beside allotments towards Shakespeare Cliff **20** itself. At the point where the railway goes beneath you with its two entrances into Shakespeare Tunnel, you pick up the grassy path which will now take you to the top of the cliffs and much of the way to Folkestone. Strategically placed seats help you to enjoy superb views back to Dover and the cliffs to the northeast.

This spectacular promontory was the setting, in Shakespeare's *King Lear*, for the scene in which Edgar urges the blind Gloucester to plunge to his death. On a bright day, with downland wildlife

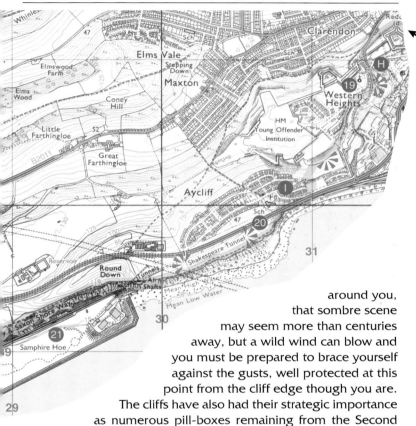

around you,
that sombre scene
may seem more than centuries
away, but a wild wind can blow and
you must be prepared to brace yourself
against the gusts, well protected at this
point from the cliff edge though you are.
The cliffs have also had their strategic importance
as numerous pill-boxes remaining from the Second
World War bear witness. Railway ventilation shafts appear
from time to time. Half a mile on, you see the area where some
four million cubic metres of chalk spoil from the Channel Tunnel
were deposited **21**. This was placed behind a new sea wall, on an
existing land platform which now bears some of the tunnel's cooling and ventilation system. Rye grass and other local plants are
being encouraged to grow around the site. This platform has been
called Samphire Hoe, after the samphire gatherer spotted by
Edgar in *King Lear*.

The spire you see beyond the A20 **22** rises above the church of
St Lawrence the Martyr at Church Hougham, Norman, on a Saxon
site, used by smugglers, as were many churches round this coastline, for hiding contraband. A mile and a half (2.4 km) from here
you pass the site of an old rifle range, now a paradise for wild
flowers. At its end you pass another ventilation shaft, this time for

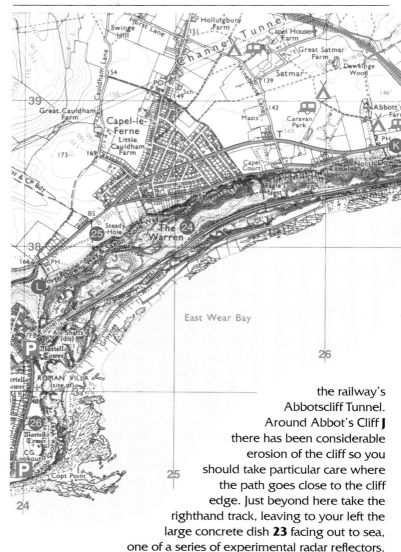

the railway's Abbotscliff Tunnel. Around Abbot's Cliff **J** there has been considerable erosion of the cliff so you should take particular care where the path goes close to the cliff edge. Just beyond here take the righthand track, leaving to your left the large concrete dish **23** facing out to sea, one of a series of experimental radar reflectors.

You now turn inland, past Abbots Cliff House towards the old A20, now the B2011. Turn left over a stile just before the road and walk back towards the cliff, then turn right. If, however, you go ahead along the road, you will find pubs, the Royal Oak and the White Swan, 300 yards (270 metres) up the road. You can return to the cliffs by the path opposite the Royal Oak, in which case you turn right onto the cliff path by an old milestone **K**.

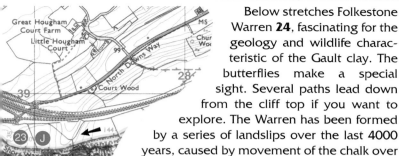

Below stretches Folkestone Warren **24**, fascinating for the geology and wildlife characteristic of the Gault clay. The butterflies make a special sight. Several paths lead down from the cliff top if you want to explore. The Warren has been formed by a series of landslips over the last **4000** years, caused by movement of the chalk over the Gault clay and by the drift of shingle eastwards. The Gault clay can be seen in the darker cliffs behind East Wear Bay. A huge slip in 1915 disrupted the railway for four years. The Shore Way along the cliff top gives you superb views over the entire area. On the shore you can see concrete aprons laid to help prevent some of the landslips.

At the first houses follow the sign past the Cliff Top Café. Beyond Steady Hole you reach the Battle of Britain Memorial **25** with the stone figure of an airman unveiled by the Queen Mother in 1993. At a junction of tracks **L** you turn right and walk for 150 yards (130 metres) to the B2011 and the Valiant Sailor public house. If you want to break your journey in Folkestone turn left and take the steep track down a deeply-cut cliff path, once a regular route for smugglers to and from the shore. At the bottom, above Copt Point, stands the first of the Martello Towers **26**. In it is a museum showing the history of these fortifications, built as an extra line of defence against possible invasion by Napoleon.

Folkestone remained a small fishing village until the arrival of the railway in 1842. The small streets behind the town's harbour are still a reminder of those days.

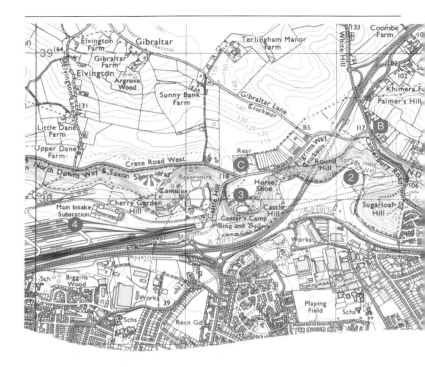

8 NORTH DOWNS AND GREENSAND RIDGE

Crete Road East to Hamstreet   *20¾ miles (33.2 km)*

The route now takes you beside a trackway which was in use even before Britain was separated from Europe. This follows the edge of the wide amphitheatre created by the escarpment of the Downs. On the top of one of a series of rounded outcrops you walk over a Norman fortification known as Caesar's Camp. For a while you walk above the Channel Tunnel Terminal, then head inland, before descending the scarp at Tolsford Hill. You then go through several stretches of woodland, some of them ancient, first on the Low Weald, then on Lower Greensand, before coming to the Gault cliffs at Lympne. Here you see the medieval castle which now looks out over the Romney Marsh, and the remains of the Saxon Shore fort at Stutfall Castle. Then you walk beside the Royal Military Canal and along the edge of the cliffs before passing through the woods and fields of countryside once owned by the monks of Canterbury. A

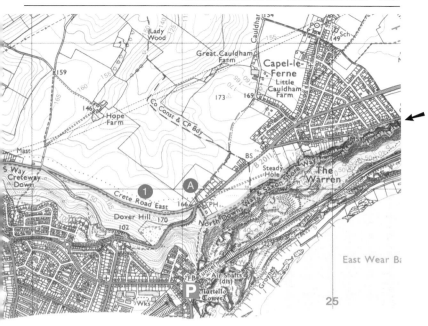

downhill walk through Hamstreet Woods takes you through a stretch of ancient woodland unrivalled for its wildlife.

From the Valiant Sailor public house **A** cross the B2011 to Crete Road East **1** and go through the kissing gate on the lefthand side to walk beside the ancient trackway. Soon you go quite steeply downhill to the junction with Canterbury Hill **B**. Here you cross, go through a kissing gate, and follow the grass path along the old Crete Road West and the slopes of Round Hill where the M20 goes into tunnel below you. The spring at the base of Holywell Coombe **2** is said to have been used by pilgrims from Europe when they visited Becket's shrine at Canterbury. Beneath the coombe today Eurorail runs in a tunnel created by the 'cut and cover' method to help conserve the natural features of the region.

Continue to Castle Hill **3** where the path takes the old causeway onto fortifications which date from Norman times. You can see the ringwork and the bailey quite clearly. The route follows the line of the old causeway, turns right above the Cheriton Terminal, and then skirts the ringwork to return to the road. At the road, beside Hills Reservoir **C**, turn left up a signed path between fences.

You soon see, stretching out below, Cheriton Station **4** for freight and cars, where the three tunnels of the Eurotunnel link with France emerge from beneath the chalk downs. Two of these tunnels are the single-track rail tunnels, only 30 metres apart, for passenger and shuttle trains. The central tunnel is for service and maintenance. The tunnel was opened in 1994 after seven years of construction work, ending almost two centuries of hopes and fears about a fixed link with Europe.

The best place to view this controversial but remarkable example of modern engineering is from the top of Cheriton Hill **5** above the cherry orchards, now lost, where local people went for a day's outing. Looking further afield, you can see the sands beyond Dymchurch sweeping round to the point of Dungeness.

Cross the road by the viewing point, turn left into the field opposite and follow the path above the almost sheer scarp face at Northcliffe to Peene Quarry **6**. From here chalk was quarried to built Sandgate castle for Henry VIII in 1539.

Swing right to cross the quarry **8** and walk up the access lane. Cross a stile and follow the field edge for about 350 yards (320 metres). Turn left, cross the road and go along a bridle path **D**, between arable land and pasture. The peace is tangible here, well away from the sound of traffic.

After half a mile (800 metres) turn left into a field, go diagonally right to the corner of the fence and follow the fence line to another stile. Now skirt the field, turn right and then left to the top of a deep coombe, then left again to head in a south-westerly direction down the centre of the coombe with Summerhouse Hill ahead to your left **7**, once even more prominent when a large gazebo stood on its top.

Make for the righthand side of a fence, then go along a chalky farm track to a broad swathe of open ground running at right-angles. Go down between a fence and a pylon, under the fine arch of the old railway **8** which, between 1889 and 1947, connected Folkestone and Canterbury. Turn right along a woodland path, crossing a stream to reach open land once more. Go to the top of this field, leaving a

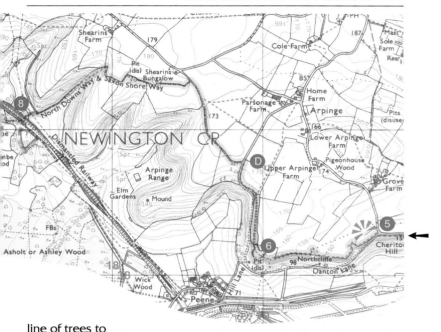

line of trees to
your left. Turn right at Coombe
Farm to reach the road **E** 400 yards (360 metres) south of Etchinghill
where the New Inn makes a good resting place.

To continue the walk from **E**, turn right, then left up a concrete
path on the edge of woodland. At the top turn right and walk on
for 600 yards (540 metres) to the British Telecom station. The
scarp drops very steeply below you on your left. To your right and
north you have a fine view up the Elham Valley. All this is MoD
land so please be sure not stray off the path.

Now the Saxon Shore Way turns left along a concrete path,
then goes almost due south across the flattened crest of Tolsford
Hill to the top of the scarp. From the trig point, 594 feet (181
metres) high, you have the finest view of all round here, from
Folkestone round to Dungeness, then as far as the High Weald and
the Fairlight Cliffs. The slopes of Tolsford Hill bear a number of
tumuli, left by neolithic man between 4,000 BC and 3,500 BC. You
pass four of these mounds **9** as you begin to descend the slope.

Turn right through a gate **F** and follow a farm track downhill. As
you descend the slope you see a patch of ancient woodland
above and to your left known as Brockmans Bushes **10**. The name
is a reminder of the family who once owned the land.

Pass an old pumping station and turn left onto a broader lane at Bluehouse. At a broad field gate **G** either turn into the field and follow the headland for a few yards and then go across the field to a house, or go ahead down the concrete lane to the road, the A20, and turn left.

Cross first the A20 to a small, moving war memorial, then, by footbridge, the M20. Turn right and follow the signs along a metalled track for 150 yards (130 metres), then watch for the waymark guiding you onto a narrow path along a hillside.

The route now takes you between trees, over another dismantled railway, and then winds downhill with tall standards and coppiced trees rising on either side. You emerge from the trees into an open field and continue down to cross a small stream, the Slay Brook, then cross the Sandling Road **H** half a mile (800 metres) north west of Saltwood.

Saltwood Castle **11** is unique as the only castle built for the Archbishop of Canterbury, who required his tenants to guard this stretch of coastline for him. It was from here that four knights rode to Canterbury, on 20 December 1170, to murder Thomas à Becket and rid the king of 'that turbulent priest.' From **H** walk up the righthand side of a field towards woodland. To your right is Sandling Park **12**.

Turn left after 500 yards (450 metres) onto a broad path through Chesterfield Wood **13** where you skirt the edge of a cutting through the Greensand. Once the area belonged to Sir Ranolph de Brock who owned Saltwood castle at the time of Becket's murder. You can see the conifers and even walnut, as well as an ornamental lake, from a much later estate. When you emerge from the woods bear slightly right, making for the small chapel at Pedlinge **14**. This was built as a chapel-at-ease attached to Saltwood church.

At the road, the A261, turn left, then immediately right, past a pond, then left through a gate into a field. Cross the field, veer right and walk along a broad field path across cultivated land leaving Folks Wood **15**, an area of ancient woodland, to your right. Here you may well hear the whistle of the Romney Hythe and Dymchurch Railway rising from below the cliff to your left.

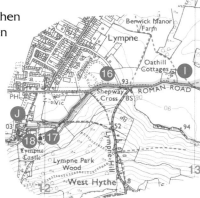

Turn right when you reach the B2067 **I**. Half a mile (800 metres) ahead stands the Shepway Cross **16** which was set up to record the work of the Cinque Ports. Here in medieval times the senior court of the Cinque Ports was held. From here you see Romney Marsh stretching below you towards the west.

After a further 250 yards (230 metres) turn left along a path to the old part of Lympne. The name comes from the Celtic word for the River Rother, the Limen, meaning 'elm', which once flowed here. The 'P' in 'Lympne', never pronounced, was inserted in the fifteenth century.

You pass St Stephen's church **17** whose ragstone tower, built in Norman times, may well have been a look-out place for smugglers. You then reach the gates of Lympne Castle **18**. It is well worth your time to visit, especially to see its Great Hall and enjoy the view over the marsh.

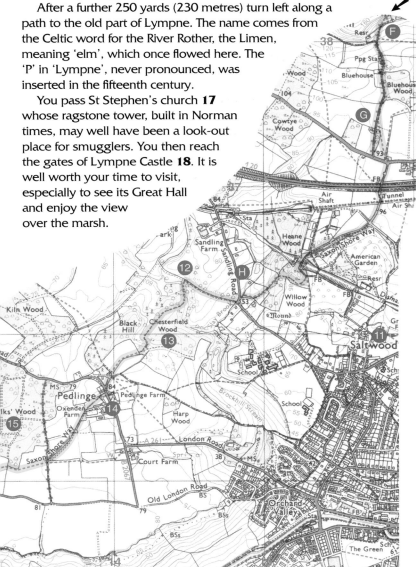

For centuries this was the home of the Archdeacons of Canterbury. Thomas à Becket lived here, when he held that position, in fortified style. A watchtower had stood on the site when the Romans made this promontory an important port. The River Rother, the *Lemanis*, flowed into the sea here and the site made an ideal place for another defence against invasion by sea.

On the slopes below stood a fort, built first as a haven for the British fleet, then developed as the fourth of the Saxon Shore Forts, *Portus Lemanis*. A road ran to Canterbury and London, so links with the rest of Roman Britain were good until silting and subsidence made the Romans abandon the site, around AD 370.

At **J** you may turn right to the centre of Lympne village. Here you will find The County Members Inn on your left.

To continue from **J**, turn left, and follow the path round the cliff top to join the road three-quarters of a mile (1.2 km) on. From here you can see the Royal Military Canal below **19**. More immediately beneath you lies what remains of Stutfall Castle **20** where a series of landslips have left no more than a few piles of rubble from a fortification which once covered eleven acres. A setting sun brings a romantic touch to a site that ironically takes its name from the Saxon for 'stout wall'.

Turn left just before the road and walk down the scarp past Port Lympne Zoo **21**. At the bottom cross a broad wooden bridge;

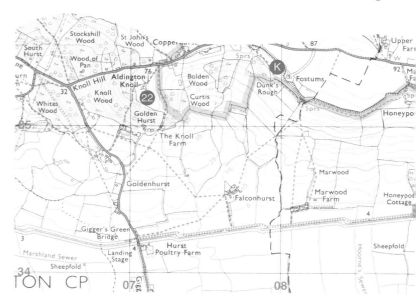

then turn right and walk along the embankment which runs on the north side of the canal until you reach the Aldergate Bridge. Here, where the zoo ends, you drop down to a lower path.

At Honeypot Cottage, just after one of the canal's many enfilades, turn right and follow the path up the hillside. Just short of an old chapel aim for the marker post to the left of the farm track. At the top, turn left and take the lower of two tracks beneath the cliff top. Turn left over a stile, then follow the track right, to walk along a broad, grassy slope beneath the cliffs.

At a post half a mile (800 metres) further on turn left **K**, then left again; then go downhill, round a field edge. Turn right at the bottom by trees, a damp patch in times of rain, and continue uphill, past three fine, once-pollarded oaks, to the edge of Curtis Wood.

Just before the wood turn left over a stile into another field, then right to walk up the righthand side of the field beside the wood. Turn right at the marker, into the woods where you will find a wonderful carpet of bluebells in spring, and emerge into a field just below Aldington Knoll **22**. This hilltop used to be a well-known point for smugglers of the Aldington Gang to flash messages across the marsh. Go right, along the field edge below it, turn right at the road, then left, 100 yards (90 metres) further on,
beside a post box .

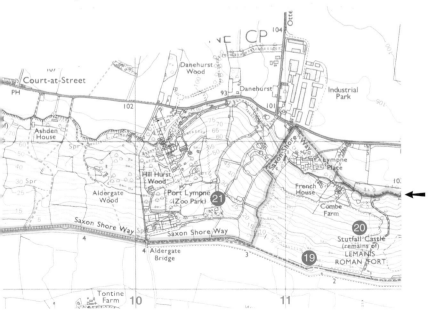

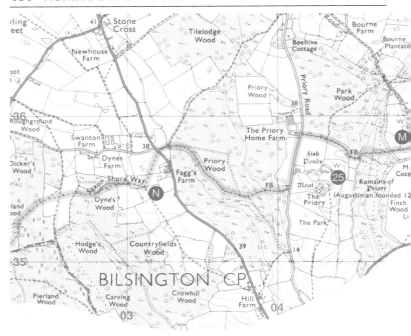

Turn diagonally left at the top of the slope, then take the path across the next field to the road. You see the tower and beacon turret of Aldington church **23** ahead, just to the east, and you also have a good view north to the Downs.

Here, too, the Archbishops of Canterbury owned land and part of Court Lodge, beside the church, was built in the fourteenth century for the Archbishop's Norman church, itself erected on the site of a palace. The late fifteenth-century church was built on the site of a much earlier Saxon building.

Go left along the road, then, 100 yards (90 metres) past the road to the church, go left again, opposite a farm entrance. At the next gate follow the path half-right, down the slope, to go between power lines, then cross a bridge and a stile to the next field. Aim for a stile ahead before woodland but instead of crossing, turn right and go uphill beside Blackthorn Woods.

The path now continues, through an area of the woods recently felled, down to a stream, then on to houses and a road **L**. Aldington Corner **24** and the Walnut Tree Inn lie 600 yards (540 metres) to the right. Here the Aldington Gang of smugglers made their base.

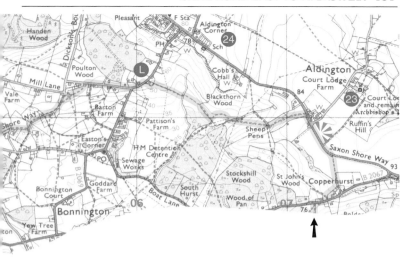

Turn left, then right, to continue the Shore Way, then look for a left turn, signed, 350 yards (300 metres) ahead, which leads across fields to a metalled track. At Hungry Hall you are invited to take the permissive path beside the garden. Then you follow the markers for half a mile (800 metres) to reach a small road. Here turn right, then left, passing Patlan Farm on your right at the corner **M**.

About 80 yards (70 metres) ahead turn right and cross a field making for Park Wood where you walk downhill through old coppice, cross a stream, then turn right and rise again, walking with the woods beside you on your right.

Ahead to your left lies Bilsington Priory **25**, founded in 1253 for Augustinian canons. Although the site of the church here is unknown, the domestic block survives with thirteenth-century tracery in the windows of the hall. At the road turn left, then right 400 yards (360 metres) further on, beside Keepers Cottage.

As you walk the half-mile (800 metres) through Priory Woods you see standard oak, birch, chestnut, with *rhododendron ponticum* growing rampant beneath. At the end of the woods continue along a tree-lined path to another road.

Here Hamstreet is signed four miles (6.5 km) away by road. By footpath you take only two and a half miles (4 km), so cross the road to a stile, head diagonally left, past farm buildings and a pond, and make for a marker at a stile between two oaks **N**. Do not cross but turn back at 45 degrees to a double metal gateway, then go ahead to a stile leading into woodland.

On the other side of the wood go diagonally left across a field to Norland Wood where a well-trodden path leads you to a tarmac track south of Stonegate Farm. After 300 yards (270 metres), turn left at the second of two stiles, just after a hedge, and go diagonally right across a cultivated field. Cross a paddock to the road and turn left onto the road at Horton Green. Go past Horton Green House and turn right.

Walk beside the garden, then go along the field headlands, past Gill Farm to a metalled road **O**. Turn left, then right, to enter Hamstreet Woods **26** where you follow a broad path downhill for three-quarters of a mile (1.2 km).

In Hamstreet woods the coppicing of old trees allows a carpet of wood anemones to appear in early spring.

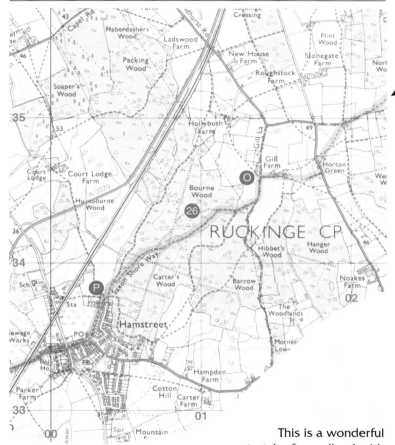

This is a wonderful stretch of woodland with standard oaks towering above you. In spring you will see carpets of wood anemones or bluebells in the glades. You will hear nightingales on a spring evening or catch the haunting sound of the tawny owl in autumn. Rare invertebrates abound here including the emperor dragonfly and the peacock butterfly as well as moths such as the *merveille-du-jour*. Birds, plants and insects are all are encouraged by continuing the ancient practice of coppicing which enables the succession of wildlife.

When you reach the exit before a car park **P** turn right, then left, and walk 300 yards (270 metres) to a green where there are shops, a phone and a bus stop. Turn right to reach the Duke's Head pub at the cross-roads. You may walk ahead along a foot-path at **P** to reach the railway station.

9 THE ROMNEY MARSH

Hamstreet to Rye   *12 miles (19.2 km)*

The Shore Way now follows the old shoreline above the Romney Marsh, with its vast area of grazing land and arable. Pasture here can seem white with sheep, especially in spring. In early summer the fields are yellow with rape, while, later, the blue of linseed takes over on the fertile alluvium. From higher up you have panoramic views from Dungeness to Fairlight. When you descend to the Walland Marsh you follow the intricate pattern of drainage dykes and sewers where, amid the slow-moving, interconnected waters, you may see dragonflies and damselflies. You will see swans among the water lilies and you will certainly hear the cry of lapwings, snipe and duck and sense the immense space and light the marshland creates. In winter you will see more wildfowl and wading birds feeding in the grazing marsh nearby. For the last stretch you rejoin the Royal Military Canal, then walk beside the River Rother towards the medieval town of Rye which rises before you high above the marsh.

From the Duke's Head in the centre of Hamstreet go ahead along the B2067 signed to Tenterden, Warehorne and Woodchurch. Just beyond the flyover of the A2070 turn left up a flight of steps and walk for about 40 yards (35 metres) to a stile. Turn right at the stile and head southwest across the fields. You will see the turret of Warehorne church **1** on the far slope. Follow the route for half a mile (800 metres) to a concrete track. Turn right at the road and walk on to St Matthew's church 100 yards (90 metres) ahead on your left.

Warehorne is a tiny village on the edge of the old cliff line. It may take its name from 'the Place on the Bend by the Weir', a reminder that the ancient course of the River Rother ran here. The present church, which stands on a Saxon site, is mainly Decorated, but has a fine Flemish gable built by Huguenot refugees. The tower was rebuilt in stone after it had been struck by lightning in 1770.

The Woolpack **2**, which bears an intriguing map of Kent over the door, speaks of the sheep-rearing which was one of the mainstays of the marsh. It saw more lively times when frequented by the smugglers of the eighteenth and nineteenth centuries.

Walk for another 250 yards (220 metres) beyond the church then turn left **A** down a private road towards Tinton Manor Farm **3**, then, almost immediately, right. Go through a double gate then set out for 500 yards (450 metres) across a field. Below stretches the marsh. To the left and south you can see the line of the Royal Military Canal and observe how the old cliff line slopes down into the marsh. Three miles (5 km) away, ahead to your right, rises the shingled spire of All Saints, Woodchurch **4**, a remarkable Early English church with work representing almost every century from the twelfth onwards. Too far off the Way for a detour now, it is well worth visiting at a later date.

Easier to reach is St Mary's, Kenardington **5**, which lies on the Shore Way, so cross a stile to the right of two tall trees, then turn left over another stile. You will now see the church tower, on the far slope another half mile (800 metres) ahead.

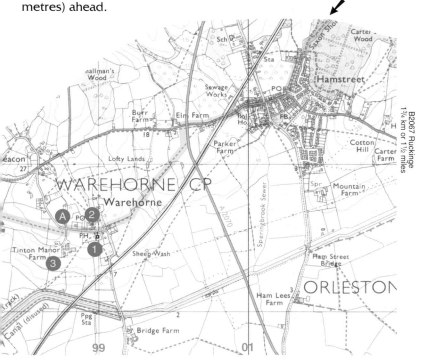

Go diagonally downhill to the far righthand corner of this field, on towards Horsemarsh Sewer, then over a second dyke and up the slope. The area once bore hops and you can see traces of old apple orchards, where the fallen trees now play host to invertebrates.

St Mary's church stands on a grassy outcrop and today seems peaceful enough. But if you imagine the river lapping the steep banks of the churchyard on its south and north sides, you can also visualise the encampment which may have stood here before Saxon times. The early Saxon church still needed defence for, according to *The Anglo-Saxon Chronicle*, it was stormed by the Danes in 893. Today it is worth looking at the outside staircase needed to reach the top of the tower, placed on the outside since access is blocked from within.

Leave the churchyard by the south-west corner, turn right and follow the path round to the road. Cross, then bear left, then right towards the righthand corner of a hedge, and follow the path for about 500 yards (450 metres) to a stile just north of Smith's Farm.

Here you will drop down into a hollow **6**, a typical wealden ghyll, which in springtime is carpeted in celandine and bluebells. A stile ahead at the top leads you to a broad, cultivated field then down to a road. Cross the stiles and walk over the next field down to a small ghyll, then up to the highest point on this stretch where the path meets the lefthand corner of a smaller field. On a clear day you can see Rye, beyond Houghton Green Cliff, where the land once dropped to the sea. At the stile **B** you can take the sunken lane ahead to Hornes Place **7**. You will soon see its chimneys over the lake. Hornes Place has a fine fourteenth-century chapel which can be seen on Wednesday afternoons in summer.

To continue from **B** take the line between the hillock on your right and a power post and go downhill to the south-west corner of the field, leaving the next power post to your right. Cross a stile to the far lefthand corner of the next field then cross a narrow footbridge and make your way diagonally across another field to the end of a line of trees. Go along the side of the field with the hedge on your right, past houses, to a gate across a metalled track.

Turn right through this, cross the playing field, then turn left **C** directly opposite Magpie Farm. The centre of Appledore lies about a quarter of a mile (400 metres) ahead. Here you will find a useful range of shops, including a Post Office and tea room, as well as a choice of two pubs, the Swan and the Red Lion.

Appledore, once on a sea-locked promontory, was the target of a succession of raiders from the sea. The Danes came first. Later,

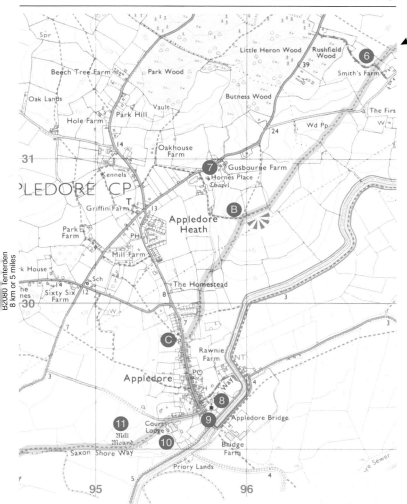

in 1388, St Peter's church **8** had to be rebuilt after the French raided the village. If you continue ahead past the Red Lion you will soon reach an attractive stretch of the Royal Military Canal **9**, where a path will lead you along the bank back to Warehorne.

To continue along the Saxon Shore Way, turn right opposite the church, along Court Lodge Road. Soon the Dutch gables of Court Lodge **10** rise on your left. Now go up some wooden steps and walk along the spur known as Mill Mound **11**, a barrow on which a windmill stood for many years.

Jacobean chimneys and the ragstone walls of a fourteenth-century private chapel

...pear through the trees at Hornes Place, near Appledore.

Follow the Saxon helmet sign over a small dyke then go along-side others, for about three-quarters of a mile (1.2 km), until you reach the bridge at Stone Ferry.

Ahead and to the right rises the huge mound of Chapel Bank **12**, to the left stands the steeper and higher wealden outcrop of Stone-in-Oxney. Turn left at the bridge to a cluster of buildings, tile-hung and weather-boarded, of which the seventeenth-century Stone Ferry Inn forms part **13**.

Stone Ferry used to carry passengers across what was once the River Rother from the Isle of Oxney to Appledore. At the end of the seventeenth century the river was diverted to run south of the Isle of Oxney, cutting five miles (8 km) off the river's length. This, the north channel, was then renamed the Reading Sewer. The list of the Oxney Ferry tolls on the wall outside tells of a style of life from the more recent past. Turn right opposite the inn and follow the cart track to the pumping station. Skirt it, then, leaving the farm track and the Sewer, walk along the righthand side of a smaller dyke.

After about 200 yards (180 metres) ignore the official right-of-way as there is no bridge at this point and continue to the per-missive crossing at the farm track. Turn left over this bridge and follow the concrete path diagonally left for about 150 yards (140 metres) to the tree-line, then walk towards Luckhurst **14**. Just before the farm, turn right into field and walk to the road, leaving the fence on your left.

Pass Luckhurst, then go through a kissing gate, into a spinney beside a pond, turn left into a field and make for a marker at the end of a line of poplars. Turn left at the way-marks, then go diag-onally right, across a field, to Stone-in-Oxney. Cross the road **D**, passing the Crown Inn at the cross-roads, swing right and follow the road for three-quarters of a mile (1.2 km) to a T-junction. There are some delightful timber-framed or weather-boarded houses on the way. At The Glebe **15**, where you have a superb view through trees to the marsh, a footpath leads down to the canal.

St Mary's church **16** is wholly Perpendicular as it was rebuilt in 1464 after a fire. It has a feeling of space, with a wide central aisle, side aisles, two side chapels, and broad Early English arches. Intriguingly, the church contains, below the tower and near the west door, a Roman altar to Mithras which may have stood on the site. The bull of Mithras is much worn but still recognisable. The altar may once have done duty outside as a horse-mounting block.

At the road junction cross to the stile ahead and walk beside a garden hedge, towards a fence. As you reach the top of Stone

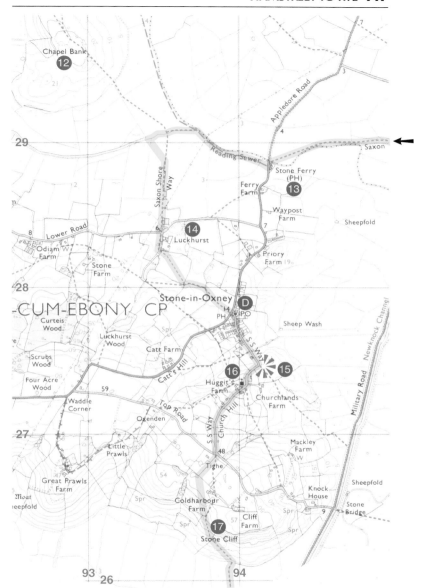

Cliff **17**, well over 150 feet (54 metres) above sea level, you are rewarded for your climb by a superb view over the Rother Levels. The moment can be breathtaking as the light plays on the patchwork of fields and the dykes which dissect them.

You now make for the canal which you can see, lined by trees; so leave a weather-boarded barn to your left and follow the path to a broad downhill track.

At the bottom cross a stile and a footbridge, then follow the righthand side of a drain for 30 yards (26 metres), take three turns in quick succession, right, left, then right again, and continue beside the first drain.

Cross a turf bridge onto a farm track, turn left and go towards a hut. Here turn right and walk for 350 yards (320 metres) keeping the drain on your right, then turn left at the Kent Ditch **18**, the Kent-Sussex border, and go up to the Military Road **E**. Here, where you join the canal path, a milestone **19** bears the date 1806, when the canal was cut. After half a mile (800 metres) return to the road just before Iden Lock **20**, skirt the buildings, then cross the lock bridge to the east side of the canal.

Iden Lock marks the junction of the Royal Military Canal and the River Rother. The lock was built in 1808 and last used in 1909. Its gates were designed to open in both directions as, when the canal was cut, the Rother was tidal to this point. The cottage was also built in the early nineteenth century as officers' quarters.

The tower of the parish church of St Mary the Virgin rises above the medieval town of Rye and dominates the quayside on the River Rother below.

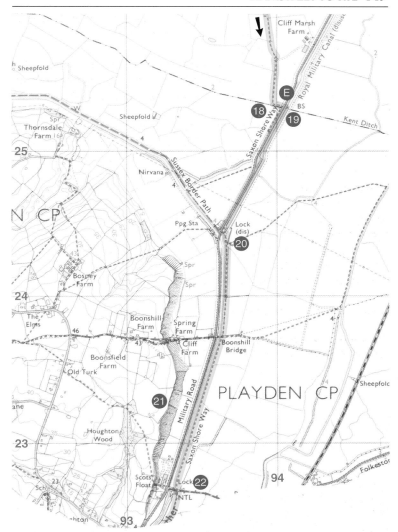

You now walk beside the River Rother to Rye. On the far side beyond the road is the steep rise of Houghton Green Cliff **21** which, like the cliffs at Winchelsea and Cliff End ahead, marks the edge of the High Weald. To your left is pasture. After almost one mile (1.6 km) turn left over a stile beside a metal gate and go along a concrete path to Scots Float **22**. Cross the mown grass beside the sluice and take the path beside the perimeter fence to continue beside the river.

The creeper-covered walls of the Mermaid Inn, Rye, conceal a dramatic past.

Scots Float sluice, first constructed in 1736 to help both drainage and navigation, actually added to problems upstream and hindered the barges which, until then, had gone upstream as far as Bodiam. A later lock was built in 1844 by William Cubitt and only replaced by another, slightly downstream, in 1986. The sluice now marks the tidal limit of the river.

After the derelict sluice of the Union Channel **23**, built to help to drain the Walland Marsh, you walk along a dyke to the railway bridge. Go beneath this and turn left up steps to a path leading to the road and footbridge. Turn left after the bridge and take the public footpath between the fisheries **24** which line the quayside and the recreation area.

Cross the road and climb the steps to the Ypres Tower **25**. This was built for the town's defence in 1247 and is now a museum. Turn left to pass the flying buttresses and Perpendicular windows of the town church, dedicated to St Mary the Virgin **26**. Leave the superb half-timbered house, St Anthony's, to your right and continue to the Lookout **27** at the end of Watchbell Street, from where you can see Camber Castle and Winchelsea. Turn right along Traders Passage to the bottom of Mermaid Street, a fascinating mixture of medieval and Georgian buildings. The Mermaid Inn, further up this cobbled street, was the base of the notorious Hawkhurst Gang of smugglers. Turn left and walk past the old warehouses to the Strand Quay **28** on the River Tillingham.

Although it later became the leading port of the area, Rye, a small settlement at the end of a sandstone isthmus, was of little importance in the early Middle Ages. It became a limb of the Cinque Ports Confederation in the twelfth century, and in the fourteenth century, after the decline of Winchelsea and Hastings, a leading port, able to provide the required number of ships for the fleet and to give them harbour. Its hilltop position provided some protection, while the Ypres Tower and a succession of walls built round the town gave more, but Rye still suffered serious damage during the Hundred Years War. Its prosperity, based on fishing and shipbuilding, grew from Tudor times onwards. Rye exported timber from the Weald and was renowned for its pottery, still a significant local industry.

The walk through Rye gives only one glimpse of the tapestry of the town's varied history and of its store of fine medieval and Georgian buildings.

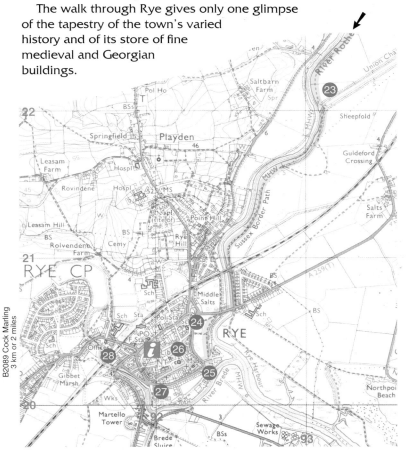

B2089 Cock Marling
3 km or 2 miles

10 THE EDGE OF THE WEALD

Rye to Hastings   *11 miles (17.6 km)*

This stretch of the walk starts beside the River Tillingham, then follows the River Brede past Camber Castle and continues alongside the Royal Military Canal below the sandstone cliffs at Winchelsea.

At the roundabout at the head of Strand Quay, cross the bridge over the River Tillingham. Here until 1928 a flash lock allowed lighters to take coal to farms upstream and to return with their produce. To your right you will see a mill **1**, rebuilt in 1932 after the earlier smock windmill was burnt down.

Turn left and follow the Winchelsea road for a quarter of a mile (400 metres), take the left turn signed to Rye Harbour, then cross the Brede Sluice **2** at Tollgate Lock; built in the early nineteenth century, this marks the point where the Tillingham joins the Brede. As the Tillingham is tidal here, the lock gates open in both directions.

Turn immediately right and take the path signed to Winchelsea Beach and Camber Castle along a gravel path beside the River Brede. Over the marsh to your left you can see the cranes of Rye Harbour outlined against the sky.

Leave the gravel track **A** and fork right by Castle Mill Cottages. Follow a grassy, embanked path beside the river. This is an attractive spot, with small boats moored under willows. Camber Castle **3** soon appears ahead to your left. Rejoin the gravel farm track and continue along this until you reach a stile at the junction of paths **B**. Take the path down the side of the field and head to the right of Camber Castle.

This Castle was one of the fortresses commissioned by Henry VIII as part of his scheme to defend the south coast against the French and was completed in 1540. The low design incorporated platforms for cannon. It was, however, soon abandoned, in 1643, because of the encroachment of the marshland. Parts of it form an important wildlife conservation area. It is currently undergoing restoration and may be seen by guided walking tour only which can be arranged through the Rye Heritage Centre.

Just south of the castle turn right over another stile and follow the broad path till you reach Castle Farm. Here you go diagonally right between the cottages, then follow the track left to join the road. Follow the road round to Sea Road **C**, and continue ahead for half a mile (800 metres). Soon you will see Winchelsea church **4**, with its five-light window, on the cliff ahead. To the left is the Strand Gate, one of three town gates.

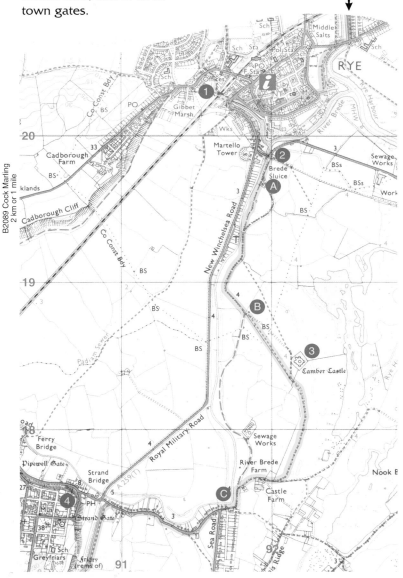

The present town of Winchelsea, perched on an outcrop of Wealden sandstone, was built by Edward I after the old Winchelsea had been swept away during the great storm of 1287. It was designed on a grid pattern with wide streets and with great wharves beside the River Brede, a much wider river then. It would no doubt have continued to be a flourishing town and a leading member of the Cinque Ports had the sea not receded.

Turn left over a stile just before the road junction, and follow the Royal Military Canal for three miles (5 km) to Cliff End **12**. Swans make their home beside the canal and you may well see coots and moorhens or catch sight of a heron at the water's edge.

Like Houghton Green cliff north-east of Rye, Friars Cliff **5** is thickly clad with trees growing on the sandstone. At the end of this cliff, beyond the New Gate, **6** you will see the fine ranges of Wickham Manor. Ahead to your left stretch the Pett Levels **7**, an area of ponds and ditches, some of them brackish. When cleared these are home to rare species of hornwort and bladderwort and you will find the lovely brackish water crowfoot beside some of the pools. The cliffs on the far side of the canal **8** are home to shelduck and from the Pannel valley **9** you may well see grey herons fly over to stand patiently above the canal. The site of the embankment to the south east, rising well above the level of the marsh **10**, is a reminder of the protection required to save the land from flooding. A disused windmill **11** rises above Ashes Farm.

You eventually come to a stile by a gate **D**. Cross and come to a small road. Here you have a choice: you can either follow the helmet sign beside the last stretch of the Royal Military Canal until you reach the road **E**, or to turn left to the coast road, then climb up onto the sea wall.

If you choose the latter route you then turn right beside houses along the wall, and either double back to the road along a concrete track by the Pett Level Inshore Rescue Boat, to find the Smuggler Inn on the corner, then go along the road to the sharp right turn **E**, or continue along the sea wall, and follow the Maritime Heritage Trail sign to rejoin the Saxon Shore Way, again at the road **E**. All these options bring you to a good shop and other facilities at **E**.

The sea wall brings a different perspective after the earlier walk, with a view round the sweep of Rye Bay to Dungeness to your left. To your right you have the sight of the sandstone cliff **12** towering above, close-up at last after so many distant sightings .

Not far offshore is the site of the wreck of the *Anne*, a 70-gun ship which beached here in 1690 having been damaged by the French in

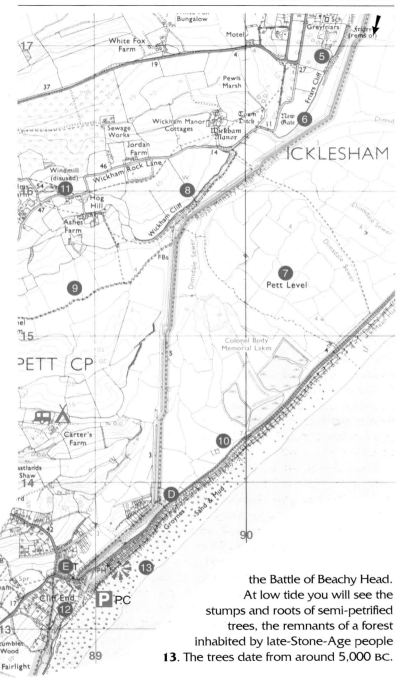

the Battle of Beachy Head.
At low tide you will see the
stumps and roots of semi-petrified
trees, the remnants of a forest
inhabited by late-Stone-Age people
13. The trees date from around 5,000 BC.

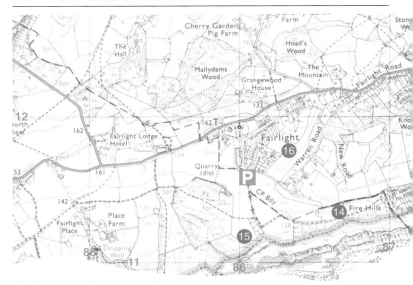

If you are tempted to bathe, please do check for the red flag which is flown when bathing is unsafe.

To continue from the corner **E** walk along the road for 200 yards (180 metres), then, just after a right turn signed to Carters Farm, turn left and take the signed path uphill between hedges. You reach the top of the slope after about 500 yards (450 metres) when the path opens up, above cliffs, with a steep drop down to sea below. Go through a small gate on to National Trust Property. Ahead you can see the Firehills **14** and, beyond, the sea. To your right you can see the spire of the nineteenth-century church of St Mary and St Peter, Pett, on the next hill. Honeysuckle twines amongst sweet briar in the shrubs which separate you from the cliff edge.

Walk on for about 350 yards (320 metres), then, where the path has been rerouted away from the cliffs because of erosion, turn right and follow the permissive path up the slope, then downhill, until you come to steps above Sea Road. Go down some steps and turn right. Turn left after 100 yards (90 metres) into Lower Waites Lane **F**.

This is a quiet road, not made up, which leads after half a mile into Smugglers Way. Here you veer left, then go first right and second left. You then walk up to the top where the footpath used to come in from the east.

Turn right at the top **G** along Channel Way, an unmade road which leads on above the cliff. Three houses from the end take the narrow fenced track, then, level with the end of the last house, go through

FAIRLIGHT CP

Farm

Fairlight Cove

88

the kissing gate into broad heathland. You are now in the Hastings Country Park.

In the distance ahead you can see Beachy Head, chalk cliffs again, but here you are on the sandstone of the High Weald, pushed upwards by the great earth movements which formed the south east of England. You can see the different strata, sometimes heavily eroded, but sometimes very clear, from various points along the way.

You now walk for three miles (5 km), at first over the Firehills, heathland seemingly ablaze with gorse in the summer. The Channel, over 300 feet (90 metres) below, is almost immediately to your left. You may well hear stonechats or see the flash of the yellowhammer. More secretive will be the common lizard and even the adder. Then you come to the Glens, dramatic, steep-sided valleys cutting through eroding sandstone. After rainfall you hear the thunder of water rushing down the ghylls, and low down in the damp micro-climate you can find species rarely seen elsewhere in the country. This area is the country's most important site for cretaceous plant fossils, while dinosaur fossils from the lower strata of clay recall the time when iguanodon and megalosaurus, roamed here. Here a number of footpaths intersect to cover the park but the Saxon helmet sign is clearly visible along the Shore Way and bollards numbered for the Country Park also help in following the route.

Walk ahead with the coastguard house above you on the right, take a path downward, turn inland above Warren Glen **15** then descend steep steps down the glen's side. The trees are more sparse here than in other glens but you will find oak, beech, ash and hazel growing higher up. Lower down alder lines the banks of the stream. Beneath, in the damp areas, you will find golden saxifrage and allium. On the far side, near the top by bollard no. 13, bear right into woodland, where a steep flight of steps bends round and brings you to the top. A parking area with amenities lies three-quarters of a mile (1.2 km) to the north. St Andrew's church at Fairlight is nearby **16**. At 599 feet (182 metres) above sea level, its tower and beacon turret are the highest in the district and have often served as a look-out.

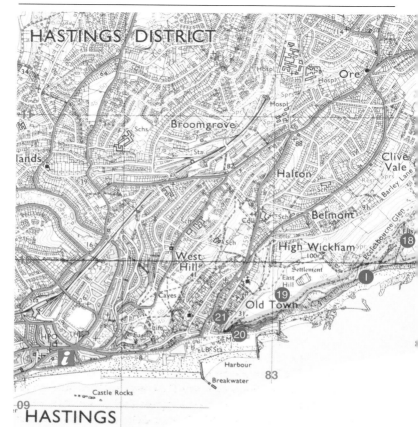

Go ahead past the Sarsen stone by Lovers Seat **H**, ignoring the path to the right to Fairlight, then drop steeply down to Fairlight Glen **17**. To your right you will see massive blocks of sandstone which have slipped down the cliff-face. It is warm and humid, often slightly misty, here, with a timeless quality, where mosses, lichens and ferns survive from the mild Atlantic period of the fourth millennium BC.

You may take a left turn down to the beach from the bottom. Otherwise you soon emerge onto a broad heathland path, with sea ahead. You can see Hastings harbour on the far side of the next rise. Half a mile (800 metres) further on turn right above Ecclesbourne Glen, then go down steps once more almost to sea level. Here you can see, on the east side of the valley, the stratified layers in the eroding sandstone **18**.

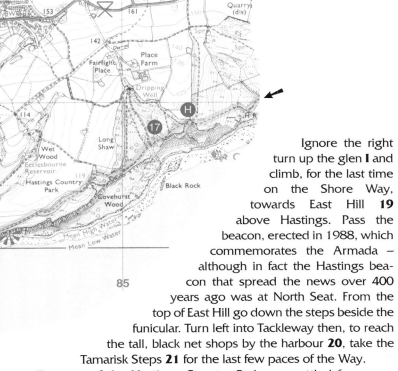

Ignore the right turn up the glen **I** and climb, for the last time on the Shore Way, towards East Hill **19** above Hastings. Pass the beacon, erected in 1988, which commemorates the Armada – although in fact the Hastings beacon that spread the news over 400 years ago was at North Seat. From the top of East Hill go down the steps beside the funicular. Turn left into Tackleway then, to reach the tall, black net shops by the harbour **20**, take the Tamarisk Steps **21** for the last few paces of the Way.

The area of the Hastings Country Park was settled from very early times. Flints found in the area suggest that Stone-Age man lived here 350,000 years ago. Much later Celts came in search of iron in the deep valley between the two hills, then chose the higher spots for safety. On East Hill you can see the site of one Iron-Age settlement, established by Celts in about 40 BC. Another stood on the West Hill. The Romans also valued the iron of the area and set up many iron-working sites. They built a signalling station on the East Hill.

Hastings took a leading role in the Cinque Ports Confederation, only yielding in importance as the changing coastline enabled Winchelsea and Rye to grow. In the seventeenth and eighteenth centuries the people of Hastings earned a good living from their harbour. They exported Wealden iron and landed large catches of fish. More discreetly they also profited from the smuggling trade. Today it is the old harbour and the nineteenth-century crescents which provide the interest. If you have energy left at the end of your walk you can spend an enjoyable hour or more at this end of the town.

The streams of the Wealden ghylls in the Hastings Country Park flow fast as they drain the slopes after heavy rain.

USEFUL
INFORMATION

TRANSPORT

The Saxon Shore Way is easily accessible from London and many stretches can be walked in a day, or a weekend, using public transport to travel to and from the route; the Distance Checklist on page 10 will be helpful in planning such expeditions.

The following railway lines serve points on or near the route:

From London, Charing Cross to:
  Gravesend, Strood and Rochester
via Ashford to:
  Sandwich, Deal, Dover and Folkestone
connections at Ashford serve:
  Hamstreet, Rye and Hastings
via Tonbridge to:
  Hastings and Rye

From London, Victoria via Bromley and Swanley to:
  Rochester, Chatham, Gillingham, Rainham, Newington,
  Sittingbourne, Teynham, Faversham, Whitstable, Herne Bay
via Canterbury to:
  Dover

Information about local bus services can be obtained from Kent Public Transport Information (Freephone 0800 696996) or Kent County Council, Highways and Transportation Dept,
Springfield, Maidstone, Kent, ME14 2LQ and East Sussex Public Transport Rider Service, East Sussex County Council, Sackville House, Brooks Close, Lewes, East Sussex, BN7 1UE (tel. 01273 481000).

Taxi services are usually available and are not expensive, at least on the shorter links.

Tide-tables are available from local branches of W.H.Smith and from the local Port Authorities

ACCOMMODATION

Detailed lists of accommodation can be obtained from the appropriate Tourist Information Centre.

The Good Bed and Breakfast Guide provides more details of a wide range of bed-and-breakfast accommodation as does *The Ramblers Association Year Book*.

There are two Youth Hostels on the Saxon Shore Way, one at Dover, the other at Hastings Guestling. A third, only just off the route, is at Canterbury. For details contact The Youth Hostels Association, 8 St Stephen's Hill, St Alban's, Herts, AL1 2DY (tel. 01727 855215).

TOURIST INFORMATION CENTRES

Canterbury 34 St Margaret's Street, Canterbury, Kent, CT1 2TG (tel. 01227 766567)

Deal Town Hall, High Street, Deal, Kent, CT14 6BB (tel. 01304 369576)

Dover Townwall Street, Dover, Kent, CT16 6BB (tel. 01304 205108)

Faversham Fleur-de-Lys Heritage Centre, Preston Street, Faversham, Kent (tel. 01795 534542)**

Folkestone Harbour Street, Folkestone, Kent, CT20 1QN (tel. 01303 258594)

Gravesend 10 Parrock Street, Gravesend, Kent, DA12 1ET (tel. 01474 337600)

Hastings 4 Robertson Terrace, Hastings, East Sussex, TN34 1EZ (tel. 01424 781111)

Herne Bay 12 William Street, Herne Bay, Kent, CT6 5EJ (tel. 01227 361911)

Rochester Eastgate Cottage, High Street, Rochester, Kent, ME1 1EW (tel. 01634 843666)

Rye Rye Heritage Centre, Strand Quay, Rye, East Sussex, TN31 7AY (tel. 01797 226696)**

Sandwich The Guildhall, Cattle Market, Sandwich, Kent, CT13 9AH (tel. 01304 613565)

Sittingbourne Swale Tourism, Swale Borough Council, Swale House, East Street, Sittingbourne, Kent, ME10 3HT (tel. 01795 417478)

Whitstable 7 Oxford Street, Whitstable, Kent, CT5 1DB (tel. 01227 275482)

* not open during winter months
** good exhibitions to be seen

Circular WALKS

For information, maps and guides on circular walks based on the Saxon Shore Way, see local Tourist Information Centres or contact the following:

For Shorne and Higham Marsh Walks; Swale Heritage Trail; Centenary Walks, including a walk through Rochester; Wantsum Walks; White Cliffs Walks; and Brockhill Country Park Walks: Kent County Council Planning Department, Springfield, Maidstone, Kent, ME14 2LX

For the Hoo Peninsula contact The Public Rights of Way Officer, City Technical Dept, Rochester City Council, Civic Centre, Strood, Rochester, Kent, ME2 4AG (tel. 01634 727777)

For the Sandwich, Dover and Deal areas: Tourism and Economic Development, Dover District Council, White Cliffs Business Park, Dover, Kent, CT16 3PD (tel. 01304 821199)

For Sussex Maritime Trails contact The Rye Bay Countryside Project, East Sussex County Council, 111b High Street, Rye, East Sussex, TN31 7JF (tel. 01797 226488).

Useful Addresses

The Countryside Commission, John Dower House, Crescent Place, Cheltenham, Gloucestershire, GL50 3RA (tel. 01242 521381)
East Sussex County Council, Planning Department, Southover House, Southover Road, Lewes, East Sussex, BN7 1YA (tel. 01273 481654)
English Heritage, Customer Services Department, PO Box 9019, London W1A 0JA (tel. 0171 973 3434)
English Heritage, South-East District, 1 High Street, Tonbridge, Kent, TN9 1SG (tel. 01732 778000)
English Nature, Kent Team, The Countryside Management Centre, Coldharbour Farm, Wye, Ashford, Kent, TN25 5DB (tel. 01233 812525)
English Nature, Sussex and Surrey Team, Howard House, 31 High Street, Lewes, East Sussex, BN7 2LU (tel. 01273 476595)
Hastings Country Park, Hastings Countryside Ranger Service, Tourism and Leisure Department, Hastings Borough Council, 5 Robertsons Terrace, Hastings, East Sussex, TN34 1JE (tel. 01424 813225)
Kent Trust for Nature Conservation (KTNC), Tyland Barn, Sandling, Maidstone, Kent, ME14 3BD (tel. 01622 662012)
Kent County Council, Planning Dept, Springfield, Maidstone, Kent, ME14 2LX (tel. 01622 696168)

Kentish Stour Countryside Project, Countryside Management Centre, Coldharbour Farm, Wye, Ashford, Kent, TN25 5OB (tel. 01233 813307)
National Rivers Authority, Southern Region, Guildbourne House, Chatsworth Road, Worthing, West Sussex, BN11 1LD (tel. 01903 820692)
National Trust, Head Office: 36 Queen Anne's Gate, London, SW1H 9AS (tel. 0171 222 9251)
National Trust, Kent and East Sussex Regional Office, Scotney Castle, Lamberhurst, Kent, TN3 8JN (tel. 01892 890651)
Ordnance Survey, Romsey Road, Maybush, Southampton, SO16 4GU (tel. 01703 792000)
Port of Sheerness Ltd, Sheerness Docks, Sheerness, Kent, ME12 1RX (tel. 01795 561234)
Ramblers' Association, 115 Wandsworth Road, London, SW8 2XX (tel. 0171 582 6878)
Royal Society for the Protection of Birds (RSPB), The Lodge, Sandy, Bedfordshire SG19 2DL (tel. 01767 680551)
Royal Society for the Protection of Birds (RSPB), South-East England Office, 8 Church Street, Shoreham-by-Sea, BN43 5DQ (tel. 01273 463642)
The Rye Bay Countryside Project, East Sussex County Council, 111B High Street, Rye, East Sussex, TN31 7JF (tel. 01797 226488)
Sussex Wildlife Trust, Woods Mill, Shoreham Road, Henfield, West Sussex BN5 9SD (tel. 01273 492630)
White Cliffs Countryside Project, 6 Cambridge Terrace, Dover, Kent, CT16 1JT (tel. 01304 241806)

ORDNANCE SURVEY MAPS COVERING THE SAXON SHORE WAY

Landranger Maps (scale 1:50,000)
177 East London
178 The Thames Estuary
179 Canterbury and East Kent

189 Ashford and the Romney Marsh
199 Eastbourne, Hastings and surrounding area

Pathfinder Maps (scale 1:25,000)
1177 Gravesend and Tilbury
1193 Chatham
1178 Isle of Grain
1179 Isle of Sheppey
1194 Sittingbourne
1195 Whitstable and Herne Bay
1196 Margate and St Nicholas at Wade

1212 Sandwich and Deal
1232 Dover
1252 Folkestone and Hythe
1251 Aldington Kent
1250 Tenterden
1271 Rye
1291 Hastings and Winchelsea

PLACES TO VISIT ON OR NEAR THE SAXON SHORE WAY

The Custom House, Gravesend

The Heritage Centre, Milton Chantry, Gravesend (tel. 01472 321520)

The New Tavern Fort, Gravesend (contact Gravesend TIC).

Northward Hill Reserve (contact the RSPB, South-East England Office) (tel. 01273 463642)

Upnor Castle (English Heritage) (tel. 01634 718742)

Rochester Castle (English Heritage) (tel. 01634 402276)

The Charles Dickens' Centre, Eastgate House, Rochester (tel. 01634 844176)

Medway Heritage Centre, Dock Road, Chatham (tel. 01634 408434)

Fort Amherst, Dock Road, Chatham (tel. 01634 847747)

The Historic Dockyard, Chatham (tel. 01634 812551)

Riverside Country Park, Gillingham (tel. 01634 282603)

Sittingbourne and Kemsley Light Railway (tel. 01795 424899/01634 852672)

The Dolphin Sailing Barge Museum, Crown Quay Lane, Sittingbourne

Oare Marshes Nature Reserve (KTNC - see useful organizations)

Chart Gunpowder Mills, Faversham (contact the Faversham Society) (tel. 01795 534542 summer / 01732 778000 winter)

Maison Dieu, Ospringe, near Faversham (contact the Faversham Society as above)

Reculver Interpretation Centre (tel. 01227 740676)

Reculver Towers and Roman Fort, (English Heritage) (tel. 01227 366444)

Richborough Castle, (English Heritage) (tel. 01304 612013)

The White Mill, Sandwich (tel. 01304 612076)

Sandwich Bay Nature Reserve (KTNC and RSPB - see above)

Deal Time–Ball Tower (tel. 01304 201200)

Deal Castle (English Heritage) (tel. 01394 372762)

Walmer Castle and Gardens (English Heritage) (tel. 01304 364288)

The Pines Garden, St Margaret's Bay (tel. 01304 852764)

South Foreland Lighthouse (National Trust) (tel. 01892 890651)

Dover Castle (English Heritage) (tel. 01304 201628)

The Roman Painted House, Dover; (tel. 01304 203279)

The White Cliffs Experience, Dover (tel. 01304 210101)

The Martello Tower, Folkestone (contact the Folkestone History Research Group at The Exhibition Centre, Folkestone) (tel. 01303 242113)

Eurotunnel Exhibition Centre; (tel. 01303 270111)

Lympne Castle (tel. 01303 267571)

Hamstreet National Nature Reserve (English Nature, Kent Team) (see Useful Organisations)

Hornes Place Chapel, Appledore (English Heritage) open Wed 10am-5pm

Rye Castle and Museum, Ypres Tower, Rye (tel. 01797 226728)

Rye Harbour Nature Reserve, reached by footpaths and from Rye Harbour

Lamb House, Rye (National Trust) (tel. 01892 890651)

Camber Castle (tel. 01797 226696/01424 882343 for details)

Hastings Country Park Visitor Centre (tel. 01424 813225)

BIBLIOGRAPHY

Armstrong, J.R., *A History of Sussex*, Phillimore, Chichester, 1978

Arscott, David and Brook, David, *Hastings and the 1066 Country*, S B Publications, Seaford, Sussex, 1993

Coote, Jack H., *East Coast Rivers*, Yachting Monthly, London, 1993

Drewett, Peter, Rudling, David and Gardner, Mark, *A Regional*

Gibbons, Wes, *The Weald*, Unwin, London, 1981

History of England: The South East to AD 1000, Longman, 1988

Haselfoot, A.J., *The Batsford Guide to the Industrial Archaeology of South-East England*, Batsford, 1978

Hasted, Edward, *The History and Topographical Survey of the County of Kent*, EP Publishing Ltd, 1972

Jessup, F.W., *History of Kent*, Phillimore, Chichester, revised 1995

MacDougall, Philip, *The Hoo Peninsula*, John Hallewell, 1980

MacDougall, Philip, *The Book of the Medway: The Story of Rochester*, Chatham and Strood, Barracuda Books, Buckingham, 1989

Nairn, Ian and Pevsner, Nikolaus, *The Buildings of England: Sussex*, Penguin, 1965

Newman, John, *The Buildings of England: North East and East Kent*, Penguin, 1969

Newman, John, *The Buildings of England: West Kent and the Weald*, Penguin, 1969

Pike, Geoffrey, Cann, John and Lambert, Roger, *Oysters and Dredgermen*, Compass Publications, Whitstable, 1992

Skinner, Chris, *Exploring the North Kent Marshes: Marshland Wildlife, The Marshland Landscape and How the Marshes were Used*, RSPB in Conjunction with the NRA (S.Region) and KCC, 1995

Steers, J.A., *Coastal Features of England and Wales*, Oleander Press, Cambridge, 1981

The High Weald: Exploring the Landscape of the AONB, Countryside Commission, 1994

The Kent Downs, Countryside Commission, 1995

Vine, P.A.L., *Kent and East Sussex Waterways*, Middleton Press, Midhurst, 1989

Waugh, Mary, *Smuggling in Kent and Sussex 1700-1840*, Countryside Books, Newbury, 1985